BEING JEWISH IN A GENTILE WORLD
A SURVIVAL GUIDE

Ronald A. Brauner

MIRKOV PUBLICATIONS, INC.
Pittsburgh, Pennsylvania

MIRKOV PUBLICATIONS, INC.
P.O. Box 81971
Pittsburgh, Pennsylvania 15217
1-(800)-851-8303

Library of Congress Catalog Card Number 95-79911

10 9 8 7 6 5 4 3 2 1

Some of the essays in this book have appeared previously in *STRAIGHTTALK: DR. RONALD A. BRAUNER'S QUARTERLY ON JEWISH AFFAIRS,* published by The Foundation For Jewish Studies, Inc.

ISBN 0-9648508-0-X

Manufactured in the United States of America

ACKNOWLEDGEMENTS

What appears in this book has been heavily influenced by my many students thoughout the United States and Canada. Their probing questions, enthusiastic interest and their love of Judaism have enabled me to share with others.

I am beholden to my friends and colleagues whose critical insights, helpful suggestions and welcome support have been so valuable to me — Dr. David Ariel, Rabbi Ira Eisenstein, Rabbi Sidney Greenberg, Dr. Susan Handelman, Rabbi Max Hausen, Dr. Betsy Katz, Rabbi Nathan Laufer, Esq., Dr. Alvin Mars, Dr. Bernard Steinberg, Rabbi David Teutsch and Rabbi Abraham J. Twerski, M.D. They are responsible only for what is correct in this book.

The appearance of this work is a wonderful occasion for declaring deep gratitude to my parents, but especially to my mother Anne Ruth Soloner Levin, who saw to it that I would have the education that would change my life.

My children Yaakov, Miriam, Yehezkel, Rivka and Devora are the source of my ongoing pleasure in seeing goodness and character and love of Judaism in living dimension; they are the validation of all I have known to be true.

And lastly I thank my confidant, critic, friend, editor, wife, lover, supporter, proofreader, co-pilot and soul-mate Marcia Faith, about whom the Talmud says:

שאין ברכה מצויה בתוך ביתו אלא בשביל אשתו

Blessing is found in our home only because of you.

TABLE OF CONTENTS

DEFINITIONS

VALUES

CELEBRATION

ISRAEL

PAST AND FUTURE

GODLINESS

INTRODUCTION

Probably the single greatest challenge confronting contemporary American Jewry is the challenge of being Jewish, fully, deeply, actively and rewardingly Jewish in the Gentile world in which we live. It is true that we Jews have always lived in a non-Jewish world even from our earliest history. Abraham and Sarah themselves, as soon as they arrived in Canaan, were faced with the difficult task of maintaining their identity and integrity as they sojourned among the native population of what was to become the Land of Israel. Early in their careers, they had to deal with Egyptians, and warring local potentates, and Gerarites. And when Abraham was to bury Sarah, negotiations for a burial site had to be held with yet another people, the Hethites (inaugurating what would be a long history of involvement in the real estate business).

And so it has been throughout our most ancient history...time and again...we have been obliged to deal with non-Hebrews (biblical and post-biblical Gentiles often called us Hebrews), non-Jews, throughout. So it was with our Patriarchs and Matriarchs. So it was with every one of our monarchs, no matter how self-sufficient, no matter how autonomous they thought they were. We had, in an ongoing way, to deal with other nations, other cultures, other civilizations. It has been the fact of our life from the very beginning that the world-at-large was not Jewish and that even in our own land, we were never free of complex multi-cultural interrelationships.

Many do not realize that even during the Golden Age of Solomon, a time of unparalleled national expansion and prosperity, our lives were deeply intertwined with the lives and fates of the non-Jewish world. Tyrians helped build the first Temple, Solomon married a pharaonic daughter, Lebanese sailors manned Jewish ships and Jewish sailors took shore leave in many distant and alien lands (that did a lot for multicultural interaction!). In all our long history, whether living in our own Eretz Yisrael or living in the Diaspora (and there was *always* a Diaspora), we were never totally free in our decision-making, in our cultural expression, in our statecraft, or in our pursuit of our national and personal destinies. And one would think, from more than 3500 years of experience, that we would finally have gotten hold of the matter, to make a go of it in a world which is not all Jewish (much to our never-ending amazement!).

But there is something about our modern condition, about being a Jew in America, that we have never before had to contend with. In all our long and glorious history, we have never had the sustained experience of living in an open, pluralistic democracy.

For Jews, for a people who rely upon experience and precedent to make sense out of our existential reality, this fact and this fact alone presents the greatest challenge we have ever known. In terms of physical continuity, we have always done passingly well. We have built up (not necessarily because we wanted to) a vast backlog of experience of getting through pogroms, forced conversions, mass expulsions, social degradation and all the other manifestations of the "love" extended to us. We have learned to live with poverty and with wealth. We have learned to live with success and failure. We have learned to live with advance and retreat. But we have not yet learned to live with the freedom to live any way we wish!

Now we find ourselves well-integrated into the life of America and America, for all its faults, is undeniably the single greatest sustained experience ever, for the Jewish people. But, it must be observed, that all the more we become integrated into American life, we come ever so much more to identify with American values, American ideals and American thinking. Overwhelmingly, these values, ideals and thinking are precisely what make America as great and as wonderful as it is and which make it, for most of us, a home like no other in the world, past or present.

But we are a special people, a people with a unique history, a unique culture and a unique outlook on life. We have come to recognize that, for all its freedom and benevolence and accommodation, there are aspects of American culture which threaten the survival of many things we hold dear. The threat we are encountering comes, not as so often in our past, from malevolence or repression but, quite ironically, from liberty and from openness. Now, so unlike long centuries of our past, we have the *choice* to define who and what we are and where we wish to go. Now for perhaps the first real time in history, we have the freedom to maintain and even enhance our Jewish identity or — to dispense with it altogether. Now it is no longer a question of "to be" but "*what* to be?"

Nathan Glazer, sociologist of the American Jewish community pointed well to this: "The Jewish religion, Judaism, has become the religion of survival. It has quite lost touch with other values, other spiritual concerns. None has to argue in favor of survival; there is nothing more important. That is the first law of life, for a nation, for individuals. It is not however nonsensical to ask why the corporate community of Jews in the United States wants to survive, and why it wants to survive in the form of a religion, when the traditional content of that religion has been quite reduced. It has been replaced, on the one hand, by the common content of a universal ethics, which has nothing distinctively Jewish about it, and, on the other, by survival — remember the Holocaust and save Israel. That is what Judaism comes down to if we question Jews about it...[it] has become the chief workhorse and ally of national survival: good enough if one has a purely instrumental attitude toward religion . . . but a religion does not survive on instrumental value alone."[1]

Correct, "not on instrumental value alone" but also on

---

[1] *American Judaism,* U. of Chicago Press, 1989, pp.xxi-xxii.

something that speaks to our hearts and souls, on something that answers to the "why" of surviving, to those things in life which make life truly worth living. This book is something like trail maps and mall directories and fire exit diagrams that mark plainly "You Are Here." This book is a spiritual and intellectual survival guide not only because it indicates how we might go but also because it indicates clearly where we are; not so much because it has all the answers but rather because it asks the right questions. It is through a lucid portrayal of where we are, that I believe, serious Jews will come to understand where we can yet go and what we can yet be.

This book operates on the assumption that Jewish men and women will find great meaning and satisfaction in Judaism if only they can come to see that Judaism for what it *really* is and not the pallid, wornout irrelevance we somehow have come to believe it is. My experience in teaching and lecturing throughout North America has convinced me, beyond any doubt, that there exists within our community today a large number of people waiting to be shown that Judaism can be compelling and gratifying. Over and over again, I encounter in my work enlightened men and women who have put together for themselves successful lives and careers, people whose achievements have enabled them, essentially, to have and to do anything they wish. And yet, I find it is these very people who are asking themselves "Is this all there is?" and meaning, by this question, that after all the education and all the accomplishment, after having "made it," there remains something unfulfilled, something incomplete. Something is missing — what is that something, they want to know, and somehow they manage to visit a class or attend a lecture or read an essay about serious Jewishness, for grownups with brains. They are astonished to find that there *is* substance to this thing called Jewish which is enormously compelling and vital. For many, the chance discovery that Judaism is intellectually, emotionally and spiritually satisfying, in a dimension never imagined, is, in effect the discovery of the Jewish identity component, the component that makes for a *whole person,* the component without which, somehow, all the parts just

iv

don't seem to cohere. The discovery (for some, the re-discovery) of that missing component is the key to huge leaps in self-understanding and, I might say, satisfaction in being!

This is the marvel I see so often, in fact, it is because of such people and the joy they evince in finding their Jewishly integrated selves, that I have come to write this book. The essays here are the very ones which seem to "turn on light bulbs," to speak to the hearts and minds of people who never thought *that* much about being Jewish. It is these students who are the never-ending source of my conviction that Judaism, when presented clearly, honestly and without embellishment has the astonishing power to satisfy the deepest intellectual and spiritual quests. My students have taught me that the satisfaction of such quests is one of the great pleasures of maturity. My contribution, however modest, to that satisfaction is one of the great pleasures of my life.

DEFINITIONS

"Who are you and where do you come from?"
[Joshua 9:8]

I REMEMBER

I remember being introduced to the glories of roast pork at the home of my paternal grandparents, probably for an Easter dinner. Both my paternal grandparents were born in Poland and came to this country in their teens. They never lost their Polish/Yiddish accents and I can still hear the peculiarities of their speech even though they have been dead many years. Yiddish was often used in my grandparents' home and my father and his siblings were able to understand Yiddish well although I never heard any of them use it. I can't say that I remember, looking back, any particularly Jewishly identifiable act on behalf of my paternal grandparents. I do not remember any Jewish symbols throughout the house; I have no recollection of any Jewish festival celebration nor do I recollect any particularly Jewish behaviors (whatever that means).

I don't think my paternal grandparents ever had a Christmas tree, but I definitely do remember a number of times when stockings (including one for me) were hung by the chimney for Christmas, stockings stuffed with all kinds of goodies destined to quicken the heart and imagination of eager, anticipating children. Grandfather Brauner ("Pop" as I called him) earned his living by retrieving items of value from people's domestic discards (= junk man, now called "junque dealer"). I recall his house always having been filled with a wide variety of interesting items culled from the trash disposal heaps regularly placed by Philadelphia residents for pickup. Dolls, lamps, furniture, jewelry, magazines, all manner of things could be found in the refuse of a large city. Pop also retrieved an enormous number of books of every description during his long lifetime. For reasons that I will never know, Pop once gave me a beautifully preserved book titled "Southern Palestine and

Jerusalem" by William M. Thomson, D.D., with a subtitle note: "Forty-five years a missionary in Syria and Palestine." The book was printed in 1882 and heavily embossed in gold and silver as was the style in the nineteenth century. Pop's admonition was "Ronny, hold onto this, it's a first edition and someday it will be worth a lot of money." I will never know whether Pop gave me the book because it was destined to appreciate significantly in value or whether he gave me the book because of some assumed interest, on my part, in the contents. The fact is, that at that time, I was not yet significantly interested in things Jewish (all of this having taken place before my "rebirth"). But I did take good care of the book, I placed it prominently on a bookshelf in my room and could glance at its richly designed spine on frequent occasion. It would be many years before I would realize that, pictured on the spine, was a representation of a Samaritan Torah scroll - I had absolutely no idea what that illustration was all about.

II

Aaron and Belle Gelb were neighbors who lived in the apartment below ours in West Philadelphia. Aaron and Belle were childless and I and my sister served as surrogate children for these two lovely people whom I remember warmly. Frequently, we were invited to dinner at the Gelb's and it is only now, in retrospect, that I see those wonderful occasions for dinner as the Gelb's attempt to create some sense of family. (I suppose I will always remember too, my great discomfort with the fact that we were not permitted to drink anything until after the meal. I think people believed in those days that not drinking during meals kept one's weight down. They were wrong.)

Aaron and Belle loved me and my sister and we loved them back. When I was five or six years old, "Uncle" Aaron took me to the neighborhood synagogue (my first time ever in shul!). I don't know why he did that. Did he want company? Did he want to introduce me to things Jewish? I remember having to sit quietly; I don't remember anything else that went on, but Uncle Aaron held my hand all the way to the synagogue and all the way back home.

It felt good.

When I was nine years old my parents had decided to move from the "old" neighborhood to a new housing development which had just been completed in the western extremes of the city. There was a lot of work involved in packing up the entire contents of a large apartment and I would like to think that I was helpful in that process (my mother has never said so, however). Several days before we left, never to return to the neighborhood, Uncle Aaron came upstairs looking for me. In his hand he held a small book measuring something like three by five inches. The book interested me because it had a wooden cover and I had never seen such a book cover in my life. Uncle Aaron said that the book was a gift from him to me and that I should always keep it. I looked into the book and was unable to read even a single word - it was all in Hebrew and, at that time, I didn't even know what Hebrew was. But I loved Uncle Aaron and if he said the book was for me, that was just fine. I kept the book among my prized possessions and somehow forgot about it. Many years later I "rediscovered" this small book in one of my overstuffed, chaotic dresser drawers (found lots of other interesting mementos, too). The book Uncle Aaron gave me was a prayer book, a *siddur*, printed in Palestine, with a cover made of polished olive wood.

I don't know why Uncle Aaron gave me the book. At the time he presented me with this gift I couldn't read it. At the time he gave me this gift I certainly wasn't aware of things Jewish. But I kept the book because Uncle Aaron had given it to me. Uncle Aaron (and Aunt Belle) never lived long enough to know how important that prayer book would become to me. I wonder if Pop Brauner and Uncle Aaron Gelb each, in his own way, without ever saying so, wanted to pass along Jewishness to the next generation — Pop, because he didn't live it much in his own life and Uncle Aaron because he would never have his own child to whom he could convey it. I have thought about them many times when I davven.

III

At the home of my maternal grandparents, who were known as Bubby and Zaida Soloner, I recall many more elements of Jewish significance. Zaida Soloner was a small business owner who worked long, tedious hours making available every imaginable sundry item for neighborhood residents in West Philadelphia - newspapers, gifts, candy, toys, money orders, thread, insect repellent, cigarettes, cold sodas, Christmas decorations and probably 3,000 other things. Bubby managed the house, raised her children and cooked wonderfully.

Zaida played the violin (he was self-taught!) and, every once in a while on Sunday afternoons after he had closed his store, we were treated to some delightful renditions on his instrument. It was from Zaida Soloner that I was introduced to Bruch's "Kol Nidre." My maternal grandparents were certainly not what I would call religiously observant Jews, but they maintained a kosher home. I didn't know, growing up, what "kosher" meant really, but I knew it meant that you had to put certain spoons in one drawer and other spoons in another drawer - they were not to be mixed. I also knew that milk and meat were not to be eaten at the same time but, as I learned from my Uncle Teddy, if you really had to have a glass of milk after a meal, you could just simply step out into the yard and drink to your heart's content.

It was from Bubby Soloner that I learned about Shabbos. Every Friday afternoon the linoleum of the kitchen was covered with newspapers. I was admonished, on a regular basis, to walk carefully only on the newspapers so as not to mar the floor which had just been washed and waxed. I never did see newspapers on the kitchen floor any other day of the week except Friday afternoon. And, as the sun set, Shabbos candles were lit. The store remained open and, as best I can recall, all other regular domestic activities continued their regular weekly course but ... the candles burned brightly and, by the time they were lit, the newspapers which had been covering the floor mysteriously disappeared. Shiny floor, bright candles, Bubby's *delicious* chicken soup and a special meal placed on a bright white tablecloth because it was *Shabbos*.

IV

My mother tells me that she maintained a kosher home when she and my father were first married but that she dispensed with kashrut when my father expressed, on an ongoing basis, his lack of patience with restricted eating habits, and all the other manifestations of culinary choreography. Bacon and eggs were an inseparable pair! I grew up in a home devoid of any real Jewish practice or identity even though I can still vividly recall a number of distinctively Jewish elements. We never ate bread during Passover. We ate matzah. We never had a seder and we never celebrated any Jewish holidays. I am hard-pressed to recall *any* Jewishness of substance as I grew up but I was sent off to Hebrew school, like all the other kids in my neighborhood, in order to receive instruction in preparation for my bar mitzvah, the prevailing rite of passage.

Everyone went to Hebrew school (everyone was supposed to) and everyone hated Hebrew school (everyone was supposed to). I will never forget the long, tedious hours spent learning all sorts of things that had absolutely no meaning for me. I remember even more looking out the windows of the stifling classroom only to see all those fortunate gentile kids riding their bicycles, playing ball and doing all those other normal things after a long day in public school. I, however, was consigned to a fate of having to prepare myself for a future moment in time, on some Saturday morning not yet designated, when I would stand before a congregation of old people (average age at least thirty-five) and recite, hopefully to their approving satisfaction, a rendition of, what was to me, a totally unintelligible passage of the Bible. In order to accomplish this end, I was required to learn to read Hebrew, work through the pages of Jewish history, be instructed in the glories of Sabbath observance and, in many different ways, shapes and forms, learn Judaism.

I lived through the wearisome irrelevance of Hebrew school and, on a hot Saturday in August in 1952, recited my "stuff" to an admiring audience and was told by Rabbi Aaron Mauskopf that I was now "a bar mitzvah." That pronouncement was my liberation - I had resolved early on that, when this precious moment arrived,

I would never, ever get into anything like this again. I was free! Now I could join all those fortunate Gentile kids playing ball and riding bicycles and doing other normal kid things. I could leave behind my many idle hours of studying spitball trajectories and paper airplane aerodynamics in those interminable Hebrew classes which I both ignored and reviled.

I will always remember Deborah Pessin and her little textbooks titled "The Story of the Jewish People." I will never forget the interminable hours spent in rehearsing the tragedies and tribulations of the Jewish people. I will never forget the ongoing portrayal of Jewish history as an unbroken chain of torment and suffering. You remember too, don't you? Unit 1: The Destruction of the First Temple. Unit 2: The Destruction of the Second Temple. Unit 3: The Inquisition and Expulsion from Spain. Unit 4: The Holocaust. I was firmly convinced, in light of this presentation of Jewish history that I, Ron Brauner, was next on the hit list of history.

At the conclusion of my bar mitzvah ceremony, my hand was vigorously shaken by dozens of congregants who, although they didn't really say so, never really expected to see me back in shul and, to tell you the truth, I never really expected to see them, either.

V

One of my best friends, of all time, was Bob Lomas, the Irish Catholic custodian of Overbrook Park Congregation. Bob used to work in the construction industry but one day was gravely injured when his Jeep overturned and his right arm was rendered almost useless. A series of operations and corrective surgery seemed never to have succeeded in enabling him to recover full use of his limb. Bob Lomas did everything necessary to keep the synagogue in top shape despite his disability but, as time wore on, he found it increasing difficult to, as he put it "do everything." "Would you like to help me out, from time to time? I'll pay you a dollar an hour and you can work alongside of me." For me, at the age of fourteen, the prospect of earning a dollar an hour doing odd chores was more than exciting and I readily agreed.

My first job with him was Simonizing the automobiles of various members and officers of the congregation. Frequently, on sunny Saturday mornings, after services had been completed, I would join Bob at a favorite spot in the park and spend hours hand-polishing automobiles and learning about life. Bob taught me everything: being a soldier, getting married, how to make a living, sex, and other various and assorted pieces of wisdom. I loved Bob Lomas and I looked forward to every opportunity to help him out, earn a dollar an hour and learn the wisdom of the world.

One Saturday afternoon Bob needed some help in setting up tables and chairs in the synagogue. He told me that, on a regular basis, a large handful of men would come to the synagogue to sit around these tables, sing some songs, eat some challah, gefilte fish and salad, and then hold a discussion. I was pleased to help set up the chairs, place the tablecloths, prepare the tables and to do all those other necessary tasks as directed by my good friend. One particular Saturday afternoon the weather was especially bad and attendance at this regular "event" (I did not yet know what it was called) was short. Several of the attendees called me over to help make a minyan and I readily agreed.

I was invited, after services, to sit with the men and to join in the proceedings. I shared the hallah, enjoyed the wine and happily ate along with all the others gathered at the tables. The next week, the weather improved significantly and almost all the regular attendees were present. Nevertheless, one of them called me over and asked if I might like to join the assembled as I had done the previous week. I sat, I listened, I ate and I observed ... grown men vociferously arguing with one another over obscure points which made absolutely no sense to me. I could not react to the content of the arguments but rather ... at the heat which was generated by the interlocution. A line or two of text from the book was read and many minutes of heated discussion ensued. I was overwhelmed with the observation that serious grownups could become so enlivened over words and phrases appearing on the stained and creased pages of well-worn prayer books. The sources were unknown to me but I marveled at the fact that whatever was being said on these pages was significant enough to energize a large group of otherwise "normal" (and "old") people.

I continued to prepare the tables, the chairs and the food, under Bob's direction, for this weekly event. Various participants invited me to sit in, now on a regular basis. I, for my part, continued to enjoy the mid-afternoon snacking and the growingly warm fellowship which prevailed. Who is this Hillel who so moves the minds and hearts of modern people? What is this thing called "Ethics of the Fathers"? What did Simeon the Just mean when he said that "The world is based on three principles: Torah, worship, and kindliness"? What is this book which has such power to excite otherwise sedate and somber (so I thought) men! I went back again and again and finally found myself showing up on Saturday afternoons at the shul even when Bob didn't invite me and even when the promise of a dollar an hour was not the motivation. *Ethics of the Fathers! Mishnah*! The wisdom of our sages ... Jewish tradition ... Torah ... all this is ours! Our people wrote these words; our people thought these thoughts; our people taught these ideas and our people loved these notions!

I think I was hooked. Rarely did I miss a Saturday afternoon (Saturday was still not yet Shabbat) seated at these tables, surrounded by elders and slowly but inexorably being drawn in to some of the sources of their stimulation. I began to read; I began to think and, with the encouragement of those around me, even began to participate in these moving discussions.

One of the participants who seems to have been watching me from the very beginning asked me, one late fall afternoon, "I see you've been attending rather regularly and it's obvious that you enjoy the kinds of things we discuss. There is a school here in Philadelphia where you could continue to study these subjects together with the usual high school curriculum — it's a day school called Akiba Hebrew Academy. Why don't you ask your parents to look into it?" Just the right words at just the right time!

Several days later I raised the matter with my parents, informing them that, as my graduation from junior high school was drawing near, I would prefer to spend my high school years (tenth, eleventh and twelfth grades) at a Jewish day school rather than moving on to the regional public high school. My father thought that the entire idea was ridiculous and he noted, with some significant degree of emphasis, that the public school system had been good enough for him and would be good enough for me too. My mother, as I recall, remained fairly quiet throughout this interchange. Having received an emphatic no from my father, I was certain that the exciting prospect of studying Jewish things was about dead. Later, when we were alone, my mother said that if I really wanted, so much, to go to Akiba Academy, she would find the means for making it happen despite my father's objections.

My mother took a job as a waitress in a local delicatessen in order to earn tuition money to send me to school. It was not until years later that I understood what it meant to be a waitress and what kinds of interviews and appeals were necessary in order to obtain tuition scholarships. Unknown to me at the time, my mother met with Joe Kohn, the then-president of Akiba Hebrew Academy and negotiated with him a significant tuition reduction.

I was interviewed for admission by Lou Newman, the principal of the school. Here I was applying for admission to the tenth grade and was asking to be admitted to a school program in which all the participants (or most of them) had been studying for three or four years already. No, he said, you won't be able to enter Akiba unless somehow you catch up with where most of your classmates will be. They've already had one year of French and several years of Hebrew.

I got a job as a soda jerk working in a downtown pharmacy on Fridays and Saturdays. The money I earned covered the cost of hiring a tutor for instruction in first-year French and Hebrew. I worked, I jerked sodas and I studied. In late August of 1954 I was again tested and interviewed by Lou Newman and told that I would be admitted to the school. What a great day that was! From that point on, Lou Newman and Dr. Diana Reisman, my Jewish studies teacher, kept a close eye on me (unbeknownst to me). One day Diana Reisman said to me, rather frankly and forthrightly, "You know, Ron, you are in tenth grade, you are almost six feet tall, you weigh more than 200 pounds, and you are sitting in elementary Hebrew classes with students who are seventh- and eighth-graders." In retrospect, that seems to have been enough to motivate me to get out of the elementary classes. Lou Newman and Diana Reisman pushed, shoved, cajoled, urged, encouraged and saw to it that just as soon as I had attained a certain defined level in my Jewish studies classes I would be promoted, in the course of the semester, to the next grade. When I graduated Akiba in 1957, I was in the top Jewish studies class.

The fellow who suggested I speak to my parents about going to Akiba was Dan Silver. In 1962 Dan Silver became my father-in-law.

JUDAISM IS MORE THAN A RELIGION

The hardest part of my undergraduate college years was the twice annual registration circus held at Temple University. Somewhat before the age of computers, we were required to stand in interminable lines to enroll in person for the various courses. As was often the case, by the time my turn to sign up had arrived, I was told that the class was full and that I'd have to take it next semester. Without exaggeration, registration was a full-day affair, and, by and large, miserable.

I will never forget one particular aspect of registration which raised my hackles regularly: multiple (I think there were 10) postcard-size ugly, mauve cards had to be filled out in detail and, more often than not, each and every card required exactly the same information I had just filled out on the preceding card! Anyhow, in this lovely set of cards was always included one which asked for religious preference (those were the days when such questions were not yet either in bad taste or illegal!) and, although at the beginning I was not sure why, the question about my religious preference greatly bothered me. Some semesters, I left the response line blank. At other times I either wrote something bizarre (Rosicrucian, e.g.) or started an argument with the clerk dispensing these offensive little forms:

"Why do I have to do this?"

"Because it's a university requirement!"

"Why is it your business, anyway?"

"Because that's what we need to know!"

"This is an infringement of my right to privacy!"

"Fill it out anyhow!"

"Just what the hell is this all about!"

"Look sonny, it's very simple — if you die on campus we have to know where to ship your body — either to the Newman Club or Hillel!!"

That wise-ass answer, for a while, was quite satisfying but still the question about religion gnawed at me and...finally...I understood why. Judaism is *more* than a religion, it is a phenomenon quite different from the Christian concept of things and if I answer the way the question is asked, I will be responding to *someone else's* category of significance, in someone else's terms and so perpetuate the gross misunderstanding of what Jews and Judaism are all about. I tended to take things quite cosmically seriously in those days.

But recollections of the experience have remained with me for a long, long time and, in fact, have become an important part of my teaching and writing. Indeed, Judaism is *not* a religion in the sense that most people use the term and the widespread notion that it is not only erroneous but *injurious*. How so, and what are the implications of all this for those of us who really care?

Let's say, hypothetically, that we were to come upon a civilization or a culture that had been previously unknown to the world. Wishing to analyze, study and understand this civilization, we would want to make particular reference to central aspects of that civilization in a way that, for instance, a cultural anthropologist might do. What would we choose to look at? It would not take us long to understand that such things as foods, folkways, artistic expression, language, law, dress, social conventions and religion would deserve our attention and would, ultimately produce a substantial picture of the nature and substance of this civilization/culture. One does not have to be a cultural anthropologist or sociologist to see the reasonableness of this proposition. A civilization, by its very nature and definition, will answer to *all* these categories and it is the fact that Judaism responds to *all of them* and that, for the most part, what we call religions *do not!* Baptist foods, Episcopalian artistic expression, Methodist dress? Mormon language, Catholic social conventions, Presbyterian law? You see the point. Religions, generally respond, at best, only to *some* of these categories while a civilization, *always* responds to *all* these categories. Simply put, Judaism is a civilization![2]

In any civilization, what we call religion will always infuse all the elements of the society; more often than not, the religion is not truly a separate matter but rather expresses itself throughout the entire fabric of the culture. We see, for instance, the enormous impact of Islamic "religion" in the artistic expression of Islamic civilization — the strong prohibition against pictorial imagery[3] is reflected in the widespread phenomenon of *geometric* art, so much so that some claim that Islam has developed such geometric art to its highest possible level. Muslim (Moorish, as they used to say) architecture is instantly recognizable and the Arabic language, the language of the Qur'an, is of central significance even in non-Arab Muslim countries. Similarly, in India (same word as the word "(H)indu"), foods, arts, law and dress are immediately identifiable as Indian and clearly seen to be expressions of Hindu "religion." Indeed, Islam and Hinduism are two wonderfully clear analogues to Judaism — they, as Judaism, answer to all the significant categories of which we have spoken. And consider, once again, how religions, in the Western concept of the term, basically do not.

In Western civilization, belonging to a religion means expressing allegiance to a basic doctrinal principle without which a person cannot be said to "belong" to that religion. In America, there are more than 900 Christian sects, providing for the entire gamut of doctrinal and organizational variation but one thing is undeniably clear — if an individual does not, in some way, affirm the doctrine that "God gave His only begotten Son (Jesus) that

---

[2] Or even, as Mordecai Kaplan and Robert Gordis have argued, a *religious* civilization.

[3]. This prohibition came into Islam through the influence of the Decalogue (a/k/a The Ten Commandments): "Thou shalt not make any graven image nor any likeness of anything that is in the heavens above..." [*Exodus* 20:4]

whosoever believes in him should not perish but have everlasting life" [John 3:16] — then, *by definition,* that person *cannot* be a Christian.   Essentially, Christianity is a matter of doctrine, of *belief.*

On the other hand, we all understand that a Jew is a Jew *irrespective* of his doctrinal affirmation (which drives non-Jews crazy!). We all know many examples of proud and loyal Jews for whom the God of Jewish "religion" either does not exist or is irrelevant. We all know the truth that a Jew is a Jew *irrespective* of his knowledge of Judaism or the degree of his intentional involvement and devotion to it. Why is this so? Simply because, unlike Christianity, for example, where *believing* is the essence, for Judaism it is *belonging!* In a civilization where the composite elements are shaped and colored by the "religion" of that civilization, it is often misleading to separate and segregate individual elements, unlike Western concepts of category and identity, all parts of a civilization interact with one another; they are conceived of essentially as being varying manifestations of the same thing.   In Judaism, foods and history and Torah and folkways and dress and law and religion are all but multiple aspects of the same body so that, in reality, a person is Jewish by *living* in Jewish civilization, by *belonging* to the Jewish people, regardless of his or her specific religiosity. This fact, in and of itself, constitutes one of the most significant (perhaps *the* most significant) differences between Jews and their Gentile neighbors in the Western world. The implications of this difference, of the fact that Judaism is a religious civilization and not simply a religion are enormous and far-reaching for Jews.

I am constantly impressed with how many times I meet fellow Jews who, in talking about themselves, say something like "I'm Jewish but. . . ." Almost invariably, the "but" is followed by something like "I don't go to synagogue very often" or "I'm not religious." Often, the phrase "I'm Jewish" followed by a qualifier is intended, I suppose, to put the mind of the listener (or the conscience of the speaker) at ease. How disturbing it is for me to hear this qualification and to perceive that, just under the surface, is a Jew not completely at home with himself, a Jew who, for *all the wrong reasons* thinks his Jewishness is either inadequate or flawed or corrupted. How sad, I say over and over again to myself, that so many Jews speak so deprecatingly of their Jewishness when, in fact, their categories of self-assessment are *not even Jewish in the first place!* When one truly understands that we are a peoplehood, that Judaism is an entire civilization, then the singling out of religious performance as a significant manifestation of identity is wholly inappropriate. Jewish is *belonging to the Jewish people*, it is an absolute and therefore cannot be spoken of in relative terms: "I'm somewhat Jewish, a little bit Jewish, more Jewish than my brother, less Jewish than my neighbors" and so on. Attending synagogue or practicing religious ritual, important as they are, are not and never have been criteria for determining the quantitative status of a Jew. Even the phrase "a good Jew" is totally alien to our culture; it is a lamentable borrowing from European Christianity where the time-honored phrase "a good Christian" *does* have meaning. The Hebrew words for "a good Jew" would be *Yehudi tov* and it is noteworthy that this Hebrew phrase does not exist in all of Jewish tradition!

While speaking of synagogue and worship, it ought to be pointed out that even here, our terminology and value-concepts differ radically from our neighbors. "House of worship", "house of prayer", "the Lord's house" — terms such as these abound and are used by Jews and Gentiles alike. What's the problem? Well, it's like this. While these phrases can indeed be found in the classical Jewish tradition, it is significant that the term which has gained supremacy in the Jewish vocabulary, *around the world,* is *bet k'nesset* or some variation of that term.[4] The words, importantly, mean "house of *assembly"* and describe much more adequately what happens in such a venue. By the way, consider the widespread use of the German/Yiddish "shul" or the Italian "scuola" or the Spanish/Ladino "escuela" all of which mean "school"! and you will easily see something of the "different wave length" on which the Jewish mind operates. For Western civilization, designations like "house of prayer" are meant to describe the conceptualization of that locus; think how much

---

[4] Like *k'nisah* among the Jews of Iran.

disappointment and sense of failure are encountered by so many Jews when, in attending synagogue, wrongly perceived as the Jewish equivalent of Christian "church," they find themselves unwilling, unable or unaccustomed to pray and who believe, therefore, that such visits to synagogue are either meaningless, a waste of time or hypocritical. Think how much of our own expectation of ourselves is determined by the culture and the definitions and the frames of reference of the society around us; how alien much of this is and how impacting these foreign misapprehensions are upon our sense of our own identity and integrity. Think of the JEWISH PERFORMANCE FAILURE so many of our people suffer simply because, in our assimilative identification with the majority culture, we have come to fashion our own expectations and standards on the basis of someone else's values. It seems to me that all too frequently, "I am a Jew but..." has more to do with what *others* think than with what *we* authentically value in and for ourselves.

There is a Jewish anecdote which sums up the matter exquisitely. Chaim complains to his friend Moishe that Goldberg, the Socialist and Bundist goes to synagogue almost every Sabbath without fail and that such behavior offends him because Goldberg is not only not a "believer" but actively affirms the rejection of God and religion altogether. Moishe responds and mentions the fact that he has a close friend, Schwartz, who is a card-carrying Communist (and, as everybody knows, that's even worse!) and that Schwartz, like Goldberg, goes to shul regularly. "I asked him, one day," says Moishe, "Schwartz, you are a loyal Communist and you and I know what Communism stands for — tell me, how is it that you go to shul almost every Sabbath, without fail?" "Moishe," says Schwartz, "you know Yossel Cohen?" "Sure," says Moishe, "we've both known him for years." "Well," continues Schwartz, "Yossel Cohen goes to shul, every Sabbath, almost without fail too, and why, to talk to God. I, Schwartz the Communist go to shul every Sabbath almost without fail, and why? . . . to talk to Cohen!"

Far beyond the limited meaning of "house of worship," Jewish culture supports numerous important and *valid* reasons for attendance in synagogue (and, for that matter, the practice of all

Jewish rituals, customs, ceremonies): some people go to talk to God, some people go to talk to Cohen and some people go to talk to themselves; some people go in order to do a Jewish thing in a Jewish place at a Jewish time; some people go to socialize and some people go because it's good for the children and some people go because it feels good to get dressed up for an occasion. Synagogue, rituals, customs, ceremonies are also expressions of the social fabric of Jewish civilization and, as such, have many more meanings, purposes and rewards than outsiders might ever imagine. Jews who know this find pleasure in living guilt-free Jewish lives; Jews who don't know this either suffer from performance failure or say things like "I'm Jewish, but..."

ENGLISH IS A CHRISTIAN LANGUAGE

Second perhaps, only to the opposing thumb, language is mankind's most powerful tool. With it we express our deepest thoughts, we communicate our wisdom and experience. With it we talk to ourselves and we talk to others. With language we build cities and states and machines and with language we attempt to prepare the next generation to follow after us. With language a person is built up and with language a person is torn down. We all have had the experience of being the target of the wrong word at the wrong time, in the wrong place and it is all too easy to recall the long-lasting pain and devastation we felt. We remember the right word, the verbal pat on the back, said just when we needed it most, and how everything then seemed right with life and with the world. Language has power. Language has dimension.

Language, any language, is always specific to the culture which gave birth to it and which it serves. Language is developed precisely in order to enable that culture or civilization to communicate its values, concepts, identity, *its very soul*, to its constituents. Don't we all remember being told by a language teacher, right during the very first class of the year, something like "the only way to really understand the culture is to know its language?" How often have we had the occasion, while speaking with someone who did not know Yiddish, to excuse ourselves for using such-and-such term (*shlimazel,* for instance) - "sorry Wellington, there's just no translation for that!"

Think if you will how many different foreign expressions we know, from many different lands and cultures, which simply cannot be rendered appropriately into English: *joie de vivre, gemütlich, yin/yang,* and so on. A language will always reflect the very culture which it represents and it is this very fact which often necessitates our using foreign terms as we speak English, simply because there is no other way.

That having been said, we can then make the unarguable observation that Christianity and Christian tradition have played an enormous role in the development, not only of Western civilization in general, but of Anglo-Saxon civilization in particular. For almost two thousand years, Christianity has been the predominating religion of the West and we understand full well that one need not be a believing Christian at all in order to be deeply influenced, and even shaped, by that religious heritage. One can take no issue with these facts, these facts are the facts of life, civilizationally speaking. What is problematic in this, however, is the ever-present danger faced by minority cultures within the world of the majority — there will always be words and phrases which the majority language *cannot* represent simply because they are not part of the minority culture. And if words and phrases cannot be adequately represented, then *concepts, ideas and values,* which are communicated with words, cannot be adequately represented. Simple, and yet profound! What then does all this mean for us? It means that Jewish concepts, ideas and values will be at risk either to corruption or disappearance because English-speaking Jews, when they speak (and hence, *think*) English, will not have the requisite terminology for communicating Jewish cultural specifics in a foreign tongue.

It may seem somewhat ironic that we speak of English as "foreign" from a Jewish perspective (what language is *this* book written in?). Jews have distinguished themselves in the creative use of the vernaculars of the Western world. It is fascinating to see how, as the Emancipation[5] took place, Jews soon rose to the top of the artistic registers as masters of the national languages (Moses Mendelssohn in Germany, Disraeli in England) and how, in our own times, Jews continue to distinguish themselves in vernacular creative output. But when we speak of English (or any other vernacular for that matter) as "foreign" from our perspective, we mean simply to emphasize that significant elements of *our* civiliza-

---

[5] The term used to describe the beginning of the process of bringing European Jews into national life; the beginning of the end of the ghetto and the start of the process of extending civil and political rights. This period is often dated from the time of Moses Mendelssohn (1729-86).

tion cannot be conveyed adequately in the vernacular, that matters which are of *our own* identity and uniqueness cannot be well-represented. The beginning of the cure for this is the recognition that the problem exists and that it exists, in the American experience, in a land, in a culture, in a social and political context which has been an unmitigated blessing for our people (and other tender living human beings)!

Instances of Jewish terminology which cannot be easily rendered in English can be helpful. The points we are making can be driven home by appeal to a few pertinent, and heavy-duty examples.

Prayer is undoubtedly one of humankind's most complex and profound activities. It is a source of unending fascination, it has been studied for many centuries and is an important, some say indispensable part of the very life of billions of people. There can be no doubt that, for all its complexity and particularistic variation, much in the realm of prayer, in its content, its dynamic, its purpose, is common to all people. What draws our attention here, however, is an aspect of the phenomenon of prayer which is quite unique to Jewish civilization and which, because it is unique, not widely represented and particularly because we live in the Western world, is in danger.

The word for "prayer" is derived from the Latin *precor,* "to ask, entreat." While many different kinds of prayer exist in many varied cultures and while certainly prayer is not always a request or an entreaty, for most people in the Western world, most of the time, even if they are unaware of the Latin, French or Middle English root of the word, "to pray" is understood to mean "to ask." For Jews, there is a major aspect of meaning in the activity called prayer which has nothing at all to do with asking or imploring, but rather with "looking inward," addressing one's words not to God but rather to one's self. The Hebrew verb for "to pray" is *l'hitpallel* and that word is derived from the root "to judge, assess." In effect, the Hebrew concept here is "to assess *one's self*" - the Hebrew verb being a reflexive, a verb type in which the action falls back upon the doer (like *se laver,* "to wash oneself," in French). Here you have an idea quite remarkably characteristic of the Jewish approach to the spiritual activity of prayer. Here you have an idea all but overwhelmed by the religious language and tradition of the majority culture — an idea, I would venture, potentially much more compelling for many modern individuals than the widely perceived and narrow concept of *asking* God for something.

While speaking of the realm of religion, we must address another matter of some major dimension (although at first glance you might not think so!). I speak of LOVE, one of humankind's noblest . . . and most sublime properties. What can be wrong with love that has not already been said in more than four thousand years of written expression? Well, perhaps something you never heard about before.

If we spoke classical Greek, our problems would be a lot less. You see, for an ancient Greek, when he wanted to speak of love, he had at least three ways of doing so; when he spoke, unless your mind was somewhere else, you knew exactly what he meant. If he wished to speak of love on the highest spiritual, and Godly dimension, he would use the word *agape.* If he wished to express his love of an idea, an activity or even of another person, but not on the physical level, he would use the term *phileo,* as in philoso-phy or philanthropy. When his mind was much more on body than on soul, the term *eros* (as in erotic) served quite well. But look at the difficulties we English speakers have! Consider how many different things we want to say for which the key word is always the same! "I just love pizza." "Make love, not war" (including graphic posters, especially in New York, illustrating the literalness of the aphorism). "God loves you." "Campbell's Soup is Love." "Natasha, I love you" (important Saturday night libidino-linguistic strategy when on a date). We even use the word "love" for nothing at all . . . as in tennis!

In the realm of religion, thanks to the Christian overkill on the theme, love, especially love of God, has become a paramount theme. Okay, I guess if you're a Christian, but how about if you're not? One of the most well-known lines in the Jewish prayerbook is "Thou shalt love the Lord thy God with all thy heart and with all thy soul and with all thy might." Think of how many millions of Jews have encountered this phrase while sitting in a synagogue, somewhere in the Western world either without understanding what they were saying (frequent) or wondering about their defective religious spirits (more frequent) because, try as they might, they could just not work up the fervor for which the quote was appealing. "Love God!? I'm not even sure He's there." "Love Him with all my heart and all my soul!? After Auschwitz?" How much performance failure has been experienced by how many Jews over how many years, believing as they have that our traditional texts were demanding of us an affect which we simply couldn't work up on demand!

No, the verse "Thou shalt love the Lord thy God . . ." which comes from the sixth chapter of the book of *Deuteronomy* really has nothing at all to do with love. Much of the book of *Deuteronomy* is written in the form and style of the ancient Vassal Treaty[6], a document type in which a subordinate party (in this case, the Israelites) pledge their *loyalty* to the suzerain (in this case, God) in return for specified benefits (in this case, divine protection, fertility and the land of Israel). In the Torah (hence, in the prayerbook), loyalty to God is defined as the doing of God's will, living lives which reflect Torah values. The Hebrew word for both "love" and "loyalty" is *ahavah;* it is always the context which tells us how to understand the term. In a Covenant/contract/treaty, *ahavah* always and only means "loyalty." The translations of Bible and prayerbook into the Christian language, English, have led even the best intentioned and best informed of our translators to fall into the trap of reading "love" wherever *ahavah* occurs, unthinkingly buying into the classical Christian notion that the laws, statutes and behavioral obligations of the so-called "Old Testament" have been replaced by the unremitting and unqualified "love" of the Christian Bible.[7] Judaism has always insisted that love relationships must, first and foremost, be manifested in *behavior*, that affect cannot be demanded and that a moral/ethical/religious system meant to perfect the human condition *cannot be based on sentiment*!

---

[6] A device developed by our ancient non-Jewish neighbors which, in some significant measure, we appropriated for spiritual purposes and turned into the Covenant concept (Brit) defining relationships between God and His people. We understand the Torah to be the documentary evidence of that Covenant. The reader's attention is drawn to Moshe Weinfeld, *Deuteronomy 1-11*, The Anchor Bible, Doubleday, 1991, pp. 330-352.

[7] Reference to *Romans* 6,7,8 in the Christian Bible is particularly helpful here.

As for the phrase "...with all thy heart, with all thy soul and with all thy might", again, a translation heavily influenced by Christian tradition, a return to the authentic underlying Hebrew concepts reveals that "heart" (the seat of affection in Greco-Roman-Christian culture) is the Hebrew *lev*, understood to be the organ of *thought*. Similarly, "soul" is the Hebrew *nefesh* whose primary meaning, in the Bible, is "life/life force." Finally, "might" is the Hebrew *m'ode*, meaning "wealth, property, belongings." A *Jewish* translation then, of our familiar quote would be something like: "Thou shalt demonstrate thy loyalty to the Lord thy God with all thine intention, with thy very being, with all that thou hast." Quite a difference, isn't it? It is remarkable to contemplate how very meaningful this famous citation can be to so many of our people who truly wish to engage performance *success* and who seek to be liberated from the constraints of alien religion babble.

Lastly, we can turn to another example which touches upon an expansive arena of our activity. I speak of "charity" by way of illustrating how delicate civilizational nuances are at risk. The word "charity" derives from the Latin *caritas*, "love, affection." Surely, one does not have to be familiar with Latin etymologies to know that, under the long influence of Christian thought upon Western civilization, "charity" is widely understood, consciously or unconsciously, to be an act of "love or care."[8] The idea is that, in interpersonal relations, assisting another person in need is a demonstration of love for that person, mirroring the love that God (Jesus) manifested toward the world.

In Jewish culture, the matter is quite different. Assisting another person in need, with benevolence or generosity, is called *tzedakah*, a term which translates as "justice" or "equity." The Jewish concept is that such behavior is done as a matter of legal obligation — it is commanded by the Torah, it is God's will. Not that we have anything against love and compassion mind you, but rather that, in our ancient concept of things, we have always understood the motivating reason for the performance of defined

---

[8] In fact the Middle English term *charite*, derived from the Old French, means precisely "Christian love."

behaviors to be obligation and not feeling. Feeling is fleeting. Feeling is variable. Feeling, like love, cannot be commanded. For Jewish tradition, *all* interpersonal acts are obligations; we are obliged to do *tzedakah* irrespective of our wanting to do it; we do *tzedakah* regardless of our sentiment for the recipient; the doing of *tzedakah* is an ongoing religious behavior which relies upon nothing other than our acceptance of the notion that loyalty to God (or Torah, or the Jewish people) is mandatory. We do not require an emotion before the act and we promise none after it is done. Our task on earth is to alleviate the human condition, to repair the world, to enhance life and people. People of reality will manifest their best and most beneficial behaviors most consistently and most dependably, not because we necessarily *want* to but because we *have to! Tzedek, tzedek tirdof* — "Justice, justice shall you pursue." [*Deuteronomy* 16:20]

How we speak is indeed a reflection of how we think and the words we use are the words we are. There can be no doubt that the preservation of some very distinctive and valuable Jewish ideals are at risk in a society (and a benevolent one at that!) not equipped to represent our uniqueness. Reading and studying and learning and discussing the details of our noble heritage are the indispensable elements in the vital, creative perpetuation of a culture and a vision built upon principles which, sadly, so much of our world doesn't yet know it needs.

I DON'T WANT TO BE A HYPOCRITE

As has been the case for many centuries, we continue to labor under misbegotten and alien notions of what and who we are. Indeed, one of the greatest prices we pay for living in a Gentile world (a world we both love deeply and repudiate!) is the sacrifice of our own authenticity and integrity through our allowing ourselves to be defined by others.   Often painfully, this alien definition comes at the expense of who we truly are.[9]

One of our most far-reaching and corrupting importations is the notion of hypocrisy. This is the idea (especially in the realm of religious practice) that partial or erratic performance of religious obligations (ritual or ethical) is hypocritical and that personal and social integrity demand of any honest and upright individual that "either you do it all like it's supposed to be, or you don't do any of it." For many of us, this bogus principle has been used to invalidate the lighting of Shabbat candles in families where the Sabbath is not observed, the maintaining of a kosher home despite eating non-kosher outside and three-day-a-year attendance at synagogue to the exclusion of the other 362. In sum, this alien concept has had the unfortunate effect of convincing thousands of our people (who, after all, wants to be a hypocrite?) that partial performance is decidedly inferior to no performance at all. Net result? No performance, not even partially.

What kind of gift would Torah have been if acceptance were predicated on absolute and total observance, always? What kind of gift would be the gift of the burden of total performance in which our natural inability "to do it all" would guarantee our failure and reinforce our sense of unfulfillment? Contemplate if you will what Christian Scripture has to say on this point:

---

[9] See J.P. Sartre's *Antisemite and Jew* — he had it just about right!

> All who rely on observing the Torah are under a curse, for it is written — 'Cursed is everyone who does not continue to do *everything* written in the Book of the Torah'. [*Galatians* 3:10]

> For whoever keeps the whole Torah and yet stumbles at just one point is guilty of breaking all of it. [*James* 2:10]

What would Torah ultimately mean for us and for the world if the only deal were to "take it or leave it"? The fact is that, despite all our negative conditioning and subliminal internalization of non-Jewish values (did I say *values*?), Judaism teaches resolutely and emphatically that each and every mitzvah (best translation = a single unit of Jewish behavior) has its own merit and that this merit is not dependent upon whatever else the performer is or is not doing!

> Because of the merit of the mitzvah which you are performing, I God reveal Myself and have mercy upon you. [*Mekhilta, Bo,* 12]

Our tradition teaches that our worthiness is not judged by the completion of the *totality* of our obligations but rather by our *acceptance* of obligation.

> Whoever accepts for himself with devotion even one mitzvah, is worthy of having God's Spirit descend upon him. [*Tanhuma, Beshalah,* 14]

The performance of one mitzvah is better than none and the doing of more mitzvot is better than less. The point is — THE COMMITMENT TO DOING MORE.

> You are not obligated to finish the task, but neither are you free to desist from it. [*Pirke Avot,* 2:21]

> When [a Jew] performs before Me a mitzvah even as slight as chicken scratch, I add it to an accruing credit. [*Babylonian Talmud, Avodah Zarah* 4a]

And the difference between *MORE* and *ALL* is the difference between a religious system meant to enhance life in this world and a religious system which destines its practitioners to irretrievable guilt and failure.

> The commandments were given to Israel so that, through them, they might LIVE. [*Tosefta, Shabbat,* 16:14]

The view a religious system has about the nature of man is revealed in its teachings about what is expected of man. It is one of the sublime characteristics of Judaism that it views the human being as perfectable. Basic Jewish doctrine declares that the very purpose of Torah is to engage that perfectability and yet, nowhere in our tradition are we taught that we must *be* perfect.

> The commandments were given for the very purpose of refining humanity.
> [*Bereshit Rabbah* 44:1]

It's time. Time for the rediscovery of the value of *every* positive Jewish act; time for the rediscovery of what differentiates us from our surroundings and time for the rediscovery of an authentic Judaism which enhances our sense of self by insisting that we all have part in Torah and that even our imperfect and inconsistent strivings for the worthy Jewish life *do* count:

> Whoever performs even one mitzvah before his death is considered as one whose complete righteousness was lacking only that mitzvah which he just performed.
> [*Qohelet Rabbah,* 3:24]

"FUNNY, HIGHLY VERBAL AND SLIGHTLY NEUROTIC"

I did not invent the title for this essay...NEWSWEEK magazine did. It is their definition of Jewish! I suppose it's better than some antisemitic defamation but how much better? As much better as "Jewish American Princess" is over some even more demeaning designation for Jewish women? Within the past several years, a spate of articles has appeared heralding the coming of age of American Jewry now that a good number of television shows feature and star Jewish personae. Having moved from primarily supporting roles in the past, Jewish characters such as Michael Steadman (Ken Olin), Dr. Joel Fleischman (Rob Morrow) and Jerry Seinfeld now occupy center stage.

Most of the current articles make significant mention of the fact that in the 1970's, when Jewish characters began to appear in prime time "ethnic comedies" ("Barney Miller," "Rhoda," "Welcome Back Kotter"), the Jews portrayed were, as the Baltimore Sun put it, "Jews as non-Jews or maybe-Jews." The first character allowed to identify himself clearly as Jewish and celebrate the fact in both an ethnic and religious sense did not arrive in prime time until 1987, in the character of Michael Steadman on "Thirtysomething." There can be no gainsaying the wonderful humor of Jerry Seinfeld or the fine acting of Ken Olin but the new media "Jewish" revolution gives us pause — just what are the messages which are being projected?

Newsweek noted, in 1992, through TV writer Richard Rosenstock, that the *Jewish* sensibility of the new heroes is "fatalistic and ironic, filled with the possibility that disaster is right around the corner." *Newsweek* summarized one "Seinfeld" episode which it characterized as "a hilarious setup from a Jewish nightmare: being face to face with venomous anti-Semites":

> Jerry and sidekick George (Jason Alexander), mistaken for leaders of the Aryan Alliance, are trapped in a limo with neo-Nazis going to a rally. Hard up George eyes an icily beautiful acolyte. "Did you see the way she was looking at me?" he asks. "She's a Nazi, George. A *Nazi*," says Jerry. "I know . . . she's kind of a cute Nazi."

Funny? Kind of. And yet, something's very wrong. In a way, my conditioning has led me to suspect that something will always be wrong when popular culture takes hold of any theme or idea of worth. What's Jewish? Holocaust, circumcision, bagels? What's Jewish? Whining wives, smothering mothers, self-doubt? What's Jewish? Making love to Gentile women, defining people as *schmuck* or *shiksa,* or *goy*?

Just what is the message? That we are as simple-minded as everyone else? That our appetites and rapaciousness are like everyone else's? That our jokes can be just as vulgar, our disregard for others just as acute and our corruptibility just as certain?

The media, just like so many of the Jews who write for them, again and again make the same painful error, the error of confusing ETHNOS with ETHOS, of confusing characteristics with character. What we are *ethnically* and what we are *ethically* are serious considerations for serious and committed Jews and the portrayal of the one to the exclusion of the other, in popular culture, demeans us, misrepresents us and offers, for our children, ONE MORE POWERFUL REASON NOT TO OPT FOR JUDAISM.

To portray Jews and Judaism on the basis of the contemporary popular image is a lamentable tragedy. To buy (or take pleasure in) our acceptance into mainstream American popular life by surrendering our authenticity and integrity is a grievous (and fatal) mistake. We Jews are now confronted, as never before in our history, with the urgent question "Why be Jewish"? Assimilation and intermarriage are depleting the ranks of a generation of our children who see no very compelling reasons for remaining loyal to the Jewish people and if we fail to make a compelling case for Jews marrying Jews and establishing Jewish homes and making Jewish babies and living proud and loyal Jewish lives, then we are surely finished!

Whom we marry and *how* we marry are the dictates of a four-thousand- year-tradition. How we eat and what we eat and how we speak and what we speak about are values that have been shaped and molded over thousands of years of time. What we stand *for* and what we stand *against* are part of our definition, and that definition, through our humanistic values and unique ways of life have, more than anything else, defined us, motivated us and constituted the substance of our vision of what we and the world at large ought to be. Veneration of age and sagacity, the primacy of modesty and scruples, the unrelenting pursuit of a program to civilize ourselves (and anyone else who will listen) through the concept of law and experience (=Torah), the ability to see God and Godliness in the ordinary and the mundane - this is what we are. To understand that in every time and in every place, popular culture seduces and corrupts and that without the identity of our authentic Jewish selves, we are indeed "like everyone else," charging thoughtlessly and headlong into moral and ethical oblivion.

COWPERSONS AND NATIVE AMERICANS

As I have been saying, there can be no doubt that language is man's (and woman's) most powerful tool. Battles are fought, hearts are won and points are earned with this most marvelous of God's gifts - the gift of language. The right word at the right time (and even the wrong word at the wrong time) can make all the difference as to whether it was even worth waking up that particular day. As Jews, we well understand the claim of the Book of Proverbs that "life and death are in the power of the tongue." We are a people who, from greatest antiquity, have paid an astonishingly close attention to the word. Our tradition is characterized, in a major way, by our devotion to the relentless examination and contemplation of the very words which we understand constitute something of our essence. We are drawn to a constant pursuit of meaning and inference and it is the WORD (at Sinai, in the academies of our Sages, in the pages of our holy, and not so holy, texts) that we discover and rediscover the meanings and intimations that change peoples' lives.

Especially in this age of facile and electronically-boosted communication where words can be promulgated and conveyed to billions of people in mere seconds, where the media proliferate and envelope our lives, a heightened fear of the *tyranny* of language is well-justified. Increasingly, it seems, more and more interests seek to capture our allegience through the often deceptive use of language. "Pro-life" is a ready example of the preempting of dissent through the clever use of a phrase which, by its very construction, renders all who question the absoluteness of prohibition of abortion as "anti-life." "Moral Majority," a phrase no longer in use, sought, by use of these semantic means to define all who took issue with Jerry Falwell as, by intimation, the "immoral minority." Oxymorons such as "Jews for Jesus" (the theological equivalent of "partially pregnant") are still urged upon us by those who wish to score PR points at the expense of truth.

Now I don't know about you, but when I was a kid I loved to see cowboy and Indian pictures. As I matured, I came to realize that there was something seriously wrong with the portrayal of the wholesale slaughter of innocent Indians (I stopped watching Tarzan movies at about the same time). As the fuller effects of the women's liberation movement took hold of me, I learned that the term *cowboy* was not particularly appropriate and that perhaps *cowperson* would be a more proper designation for that particular profession (shoeshine person, newspaper person, good old person, etc.) Just joking! In fact, our growing sensitivity to sexism in language is, in truth, one of the great benefits of our recent social awakening. We now understand just how much sexist language has served to deny the integrity and validity of females in our society. But there are limits!

Of late, the term "Native American" has found increasing vogue among many of our fellow citizens and as I contemplate the term I become more and more uncomfortable with its implications. Perhaps there is a designation a bit more felicitous than "Indian" but, to tell you the truth "Native American" is highly offensive to me. I, too, am a Native American as are the hundreds of millions of people born in the United States. Our relationship with this country surely should not be defined on the basis of how long we have been here - there is no room for the concept of the priority of belonging and a trans-Bering Sea migration in antiquity doesn't seem to me to bestow any particular beneficial distinctions on the descendants of those trekkers, no greater distinction than the fact that my forbears came here through a transatlantic migration from Poland. Our commitment to the liberation of the oppressed should not be allowed to cloud our view of the serious implications inherent in the language we all too often carelessly use.

WOLFGANG PUCK ON 'TRADITION'

"And those things do best please me that befall prepost'rously"
(*Midsummer-Night's Dream,* Act III, scene 2, line 120)

This was so bad, I just have to tell you about it! Some while ago, the New York Times ran a lengthy article featuring the world-renowned chef and restauranteur Wolfgang Puck and the preparations he and his wife were making for a large seder at Spago, near Sunset Boulevard (that's right, Spago). Usually, I would skip over an article like this in favor of something a bit more worthy (or interesting or significant or whatever) but what caught my eye was the use of the words Tradition and Seder which appeared prominently.

One of the decided deficits of strong Jewish-conditioning is that your heightened visual and aural sensitivity lead you to see and hear many more things than you would really want to (often with resultant nausea and depression). But, here's the point...what do the words Seder and Tradition really mean? Puck tells us that he is simply "a nice Catholic boy from Austria" who got into "the seder business by marrying Barbara Lazaroff who describes herself as 'just a Jewish broad from the Bronx'" (whew!). Lazaroff thought that people without families ought to have a place to "celebrate Passover" (her words). All the rest of the article focuses singularly on food (to suggest, I suppose, that Liberation from Egypt was, in essence, Liberation from inferior cuisine). We learn that Spago's matzah dough is mixed in the restaurant's pizza machine, that the matzah balls are cooked with clarified butter and that the potato latkes are served under paté de foie gras ("as close to chopped chicken liver as Mr. Puck proposed to get . . ."). Puck bakes his matzot with chili flakes, he says, "because we're close to Mexico and there must be a few Jews from Mexico." Further, exhorts Puck, he is "happy to follow tradition, he insists on it, but not to the detriment of taste — sometimes tradition can get boring."

I suppose anything can be made to mean anything and that as long as one uses the familiar labels, meaning can be twisted in any direction. How much of what we love and venerate can be distorted to reflect the ignorance and spiritual vacuity of large sectors of the American Jewish community? If this is *Jewish,* then I don't wonder at all why many of our inquiring and sensitive people (children, too) find no compelling response to the question "Why Be Jewish?" The Times article ended with this:

> As the seder drew to a close, the guests packed their doggie bags of matzohs and cookies and streamed out, one satisfied customer shouting: "Next year in Spago!"

SACKS APPEAL AND THE JEWS

It was love at first read! I came across a copy of *Awakenings,* before the excellent film, based on that book, was produced. Perhaps it was some blurb on the front or back of the book, I don't really remember, but somehow I started reading and was completely unable to put the book down until I had finished every last word. I was overcome (still am) by the beauty of the writing, by the profundity of insight, by the exquisite gentleness and compassion shown by Dr. Oliver Sacks to his patients. Here was a physician, poet, writer, counselor, humanist all wrapped up in one and my pleasure at reading his work was unbounded.

Truth be told, as I read, my chauvinism also kicked in, as it always does. This guy is terrific! His book is one of the best I have *ever* read! The insights and sensitivities here are remarkable! How could any one person be so brilliant, so on-target, so profound? . . . he *must* be Jewish! (that happens to you, too, sometimes, doesn't it?) . . . I read and I read and I read — totally absorbing everything he had to say while, at the same time, I searched for any clue whatsoever that Sacks was indeed one of our people. Try as I might, I could find nothing at all in *Awakenings* and by the time I finished the book, I reluctantly but honestly reminded myself that no, we Jews don't have any monopoly on the kind of talents and expertise reflected in Sacks' work; wisdom and brilliance and talent and insight are evenly distributed throughout the world, among *all* God's creatures and Sacks serves to prove that to us.

But still, I couldn't quite help feeling that, despite all my good intention and objective reflection on the subject, somehow Oliver Sacks *had* to be Jewish. I continued to read any and every popular work he had produced, with about the same level of enjoyment as the first reading and still, search though I might, I found not one clue, not one intimation, not one graphic suggestion as to the religious/cultural identity of the author. I gave up! Indeed, I repeated to myself, you don't *have* to be Jewish to be a brilliant physician!

Some time later, on a flight to a speaking engagement, I was leafing through a copy of USAir Magazine and what to my wondering eyes should appear but an article entitled "The Wide, Wide World of Oliver Sacks." Eagerly I read the opening "'I was a terrible Santa Claus,' says the man who is, physically, a dead ringer for old Saint Nick . . ." and I settled down with what was certain to be a pleasant respite with one of my favorite writers. The article continued with a comment by Robin Williams describing Dr. Sacks as "Schweitzer and Schwarzenegger — incredibly shy, but aggressive in how he pursues an idea" and I revelled in learning more and more about this unusual physician. Santa Claus. Schweitzer. Oliver Wolf Sacks (*Wolf?*) . . . and then, like the proverbial ton of bricks, the article informed me that " . . . Oliver Sacks' unique language, sensibility, and culture began to form as the youngest child of two doctors, Samuel and Muriel Elsie (Landau) Sacks . . . he has a vision of his father, a general practitioner who saw patients into his 90's, away from medicine, poring over the Talmud — rabbinical commentaries on Scripture and law famous for the circles of analysis which bring them to their precise arguments. . . ."

Aha!, finally, just what I had been looking for — not absolutely definitive, but good enough cause for positive presumption — Oliver Sacks is a Jew! That was it. No other hint in the entire six-page article. However, my ethnic/familial pride was satisfied with yet this newest attestation to the wonderful heights to which our people can aspire and succeed. But wait . . . everything's not quite alright. How come in reading five books by Sacks, I could never discover what I just read as a small paragraph in an airline magazine? How come in hundreds of pages of wonderful writing by an enormously talented neurologist I could not find *one single, unambiguous* reference to the Jewish cultural roots and values of the writer? I do indeed think something's wrong.

Yes, ultimately, sublime talent, insight and ability notwithstanding, a person doesn't "have it all together" until his Jewish component is also integrated into his work. Somehow, someway, each of us is bound to reflect our Jewishness in what we do, each of us must feel the compelling desire to make our Jewishness and what we do for a living, closely linked. Somehow, whoever we are and whatever our training and whatever our pursuits and whatever the worlds we traverse - the Jewish tradition, Torah, Jewish morality, Jewish values have to be observable components of our activity (=Kiddush Hashem[10]). When they are not, no matter what heights of professional success or public acclaim we might achieve, we are not complete and integrated beings, we have not come to terms with the fullness of who and what we are and, consequently, in ways we might not always be able to discern, our pursuits and accomplishments are defective and flawed.

How sad that Robin Williams saw fit to associate Sacks with Dr. Albert Schweitzer and not with, say Dr. Waldemar Haffkine. If Sacks' life and work are more like Schweitzer's, if first associations draw more from Christian models (as sublime and praiseworthy as they are!) than Jewish ones, then something is wrong! I await a fully awakened Oliver Wolf Sacks!

---

[10] Literally, in Hebrew, "sanctification of The Name (of God)." This term is a classical value-concept which is applied to a number of circumstances: to suffer death rather than abandon God or the Jewish people; to conduct one's affairs in accordance with the demands of Torah; to persevere in one's Jewishness despite hostility or rejection by the Gentile world.

"'TIS THE SEASON. . ."

I always look forward to the approach of Christmas! I enjoy the thought that hundreds of thousands of our people will be growingly uncomfortable as the world around us prepares for one of its fondest celebrations. I wish even more hundreds of thousands of our people would become uncomfortable as the season of the Nativity draws near. I am grateful for the existence of Christmas and I believe it is one of the potentially most far-reaching contributions the Christian world could ever make to contemporary American Judaism. Whaaat? Are you serious? Have you gone off the deep end?

No deep end at all, just some serious reflection on the realities of Diaspora residence and the consequences of choosing to live in a Gentile world. Unfortunately, there seem to be too few stimuli for our thinking seriously about who we are, what we want for ourselves and our families. Only infrequently are we prodded into questioning the substance of our own identity. As life in the Velvet Diaspora continues to offer us its pleasures and accomplishments, we encounter few occasions to ask the questions that *really* count. The seductive quality of American life and culture is ready to take hold of all of us and I find it sobering myself to recall the time in junior high school when I enthusiastically sang in the school choir and blithely intoned the verses to "Silent Night", "Come All Ye Faithful" and "Little Town of Bethlehem". Those were the days too, when my homeroom teachers, committed to the universality of biblical literature, began class with a reading of "The Lord's Prayer" (*Matthew* 6:9 ff.) or, don't you remember too, "When I was a child, I spake as a child, I understood as a child . . ." (*I Corinthians* 13:11), believing that such recitations would contribute mightily to my becoming a good American with no thought that those verses contained ideas *contrary* to Jewish doctrine.

Christmas is coming and, once again, the questions are flying. Should I participate in the office Christmas party? What should I do, or not do about the Xmas (some would call them "seasonal") decorations in my child's public school classroom? If Hanukkah decorations are given equal time, that makes it okay, doesn't it? Isn't a Christmas tree on the steps of the county building just part of the celebration of winter? And, by the way, there *is* a menorah right next to it (which, conveniently, the Supreme Court has determined to be a *secular* symbol). Why continue to get hung up on those fine points which only serve to separate people, exacerbate ethnic frictions, generate ill-will and keep the ACLU so busy? There's room for all of us and even the Supreme Court has been moving in the direction of accommodation rather than strict separation when it comes to matters of church and state.

For many of our people, the coming holiday season is the perfect time for re-emphasizing what we all have in common, what we all share in the fullness of the "Judeo-Christian tradition" (we'll talk about this spurious label another time). A case in point is an article which appeared a few years back in the *Philadelphia Inquirer.* Its author, Melissa Dribben, admitted that "December can be a rough month for those of us in the minorities" and then went on to remark that "For weeks, my kids had been obsessed with the vision of a tree. My husband and I gave in somewhere between 'Because we're Jewish' and 'It's not like we're asking for a manger.' Decorations were tricky. We tried to find a Star of David for the top but settled on a few pink balls, a reindeer troll, a toy soldier and one cheap silver garland. . . .My relatives may be horrified, but my children are in heaven. Among the presents they will find tomorrow when they sneak downstairs with their hearts thumping is a giant dreidel." Anything for the children!

Melissa Dribben capitulated. Many other fellow-Jews will capitulate ("we're Americans"; "we can't impose our prejudices on our children"; "you're really attaching much more significance to this than it really deserves.") But many others will stop and ask themselves some probing questions, thanks to Christmas, and will wrestle with some troubling dilemmas. They will come to understand that worthy ideals have a cost and that all significant choices *will* have significant consequences. They will ponder the truth that American popular culture's excessive stress on "our children's happiness" contributes profoundly to the family's moral decay (no matter what religion you are) and that maybe, just maybe, there are some good reasons why a person might want to remain Jewish and raise a Jewish family.

What a wonderful time of the year to contemplate Judaism's messages that God doesn't have a Son, but that we are all God's children. That the perfecting of this world is far more significant than earning admission to the next (which Jews are assured of, anyway) and that the salvation of the *group* is what will save the world, not the salvation of the *individual*. That God has created us with pure souls, untainted with any polluting "Original Sin" and that how we *act* is far more significant than what we *say*. That one doesn't have to be Jewish to be a "mensch" and that there are multiple varieties of "Truth". That the only ones who "die for our sins" are the people we kill with our acts of violence and injustice and that it is *always* possible for a person to mend his ways and come back to doing God's will.

Choosing to live in the Diaspora, choosing to live in a Gentile world means that we will lose some of our people to assimilation. Choosing to live in a Gentile world means that there will be incessant pressures upon us (even out of good will) to become homogenized. Choosing to live in a Gentile world means that the ideals and values we stand for will be constantly exposed to danger. Choosing to reside in a Gentile world means, if we stand for anything at all, that we will endlessly observe with anguish our children's alienation and differentiation from the world around them. Choosing to live in a Gentile world means we have to make decisions. We have to decide what in our lives and values and identities is and is not negotiable as we make the accommodations necessary for living in that world. Choosing to dwell in a Gentile world means that only Jews who live proud and loyal Jewish lives are, ultimately, the most determinant models for those who come after us and that the *joy* and *happiness* of living rich, substantial Jewish lives still give us the power to resist moral oblivion and hold fast to views of life and meaning and purpose the entire world cannot do without.

A merry Christmas to all our Gentile friends and neighbors whose celebration at this season of the year is the fruit of millennia-long Jewish tenacity and refusal to relinquish a vision.

". . . I HAVE CALLED YOU BY NAME, YOU ARE MINE."[11]

Why do the Greeks and Romans get all the credit? It seems to me patently unfair that every time a new medical discovery is made, it invariably gets a Greek or Latin name. Now I know this is a long-respected convention of medicine and science and I suppose change in this area, even the kind of change prompted by solid logic and flawless reasoning, will not come easily but I can't help reflecting upon this important arena for Jewish concern. I have often spoken of the lamentable state of affairs where prominent Jews, who have contributed so significantly to American life represent a Jewishness which is all but invisible. We have a deplorable history, here in America, of obscuring, in many avenues of our activity, the Jewish identity both of the things we do and of the doers (half a billion dollars for public education and not a single word about Walter Annenberg's people!) All the world should know that we Jews continue to confer, way out of proportion to our numbers, vast benefits for the well-being of humankind.

There's hope! Scientists have recently discovered a natural antibiotic in sharks which holds enormous promise for human medicine. Called squalamine (from the Latin *Squalis acanthias,* dogfish shark), this powerful killer of fungi, bacteria and parasites has the potential for saving millions of lives in the future. The discovery of squalamine was made by a research team headed by Dr. Michael A. Zasloff, a proud and loyal Jew. He first worked with the skin of frogs and discovered a substance that inhibits infection and inflammation in these amphibians. Because the substance has such enormous protective qualities, Zasloff named it *magainin,* from the Hebrew word for "shield." Derivatives of

---

[11] *Isaiah* 43:1.

magainin are now being tested as antibiotics for impetigo and diabetic ulcers at Zasloff's Magainin Pharmaceuticals in Plymouth Meeting, Pa. Next step? Let's see if we can move from *squalamine* to *refuine,* from the Hebrew word for "healing" and suggestive of *Exodus* 15:26 ". . . for I the *Lord* am your healer." Who was Aesculapius anyway?

VALUES

*"...Making the Torah clear and giving the meaning
so that the people can understand..."*
[Nehemiah 8:8]

WHY BE JEWISH?

There have not been many times in the history of the Jewish people when a question such as this *had* to be asked. For most of us, for most of the long and wonderful history of our people, the response to this question was either self-evident or was decided for us by our oppressors. The American experience in the life of the Jewish people comprises a set of phenomena which, in large measure, we have never encountered before. We now live in a Gentile world which accommodates us, we live in a society which we love and, importantly, most of the barriers to assimilation which confronted us in millennia past no longer exist. In brief, we are challenged as never before by a world around us which we find felicitous, attractive and largely compatible with what we *believe* to be Jewish life and values. No longer are we Jewish because virulent antisemites point their bloody fingers at us. No longer are we Jewish because church homilies denigrate and vilify us to mindless audiences of simple worshippers. No longer are we Jewish because we *suffer* or because we are reviled. No longer are we Jewish because we have no *choice.* At last, it is possible for us to escape our Jewishness if we care to, given the social, economic, political, educational and religious mobility and freedom we all enjoy. We can, if we so choose, disappear (and, indeed, many have chosen that option!).

In America, we have "arrived" and we have discovered that not all Gentiles are "goyim" and some, who used to be "goyim" are now our wives and husbands. We have discovered a world which we do not repudiate and we have discovered a world into which we can invest heart and soul and body and mind and spirit. But very little in our past can help us deal, in terms of PRECEDENT, with the American phenomenon. Now we are subject to the influences of popular culture in exceptional ways. Now, for the first time in a long time, we possess the means to pursue (and achieve!) our ancient aspiration to be "... like the nations around us."

Things really have changed! No more can we take for granted that our children will love and identify with the heritage of their elders or abstain from dating and marrying non-Jews — not now that we have discovered that we Jews have no monopoly on refinement or civility or menschlichkeit or intelligence or morality. No longer can we take for granted that all that we are and all that we represent are superior to and more desirable than the alternatives around us. No longer can we simply assume that Judaism is the only way to go. No longer can we unthinkingly presume that the reasons for being Jewish are both compelling and self-evident. Now as never before we *must* be able to formulate, both for ourselves and for those we care about, reasonable, meaningful, honest responses to the question "Why be Jewish?"

In America, everything is open for discussion (just think of your favorite talk show), everything can be examined before the camera lens (X-rated, etc.) and everything is subject to question. We still live under the influence of the let-it-all-hang-out ethic and one searches in vain for topics which, for one good reason or another, even Geraldo Rivera wouldn't touch. So...if no question is off limits, if no topic is out of bounds and if no inquiry is unwarranted, what will we respond when our sons and daughters want to know *why* we oppose dating and intermarriage (and we DO oppose, even those of us whose children have gone their own way!). We have spent many decades polishing the theme of what we Americans all have in common. Articles and books galore extol the virtues of the "Judeo-Christian Tradition" and more than a few invocations, graduation speeches and brotherhood gatherings have sought to promote the common ground of "The fatherhood of God and the brotherhood of man." With so much in *common,* why be *different?*

1.

Thus taught Rabbi Shimon bar Yohai: men were sitting in a boat and one of them took a drill and

began to bore a hole in the floor of the boat under his feet. His fellow passengers said to him: "What are you doing?" "What is it your matter, am I not drilling a hole under my own seat?" "Yes," they responded, "but when the water comes up it will drown us all!"
(Leviticus Rabbah 4:6)[12]

From earliest times, Judaism has focused upon the community, the group, as the unit of significance for making sense out of life's purpose and the nature of reality. Family, clan, tribe, peoplehood - the biblical record is replete with references to corporate entities when it speaks about the organization of society, human relations, behavioral norms and covenant.

The idea that there exists a legally defined relationship between God and humankind and God and the Jewish people goes back to the earliest expressions of Jewish thought. Noah was promised by God that no flood would ever again destroy humanity and the rainbow was designated as the "signature" on that divine promise. Abraham and his descendants were promised unconditional fertility, territory, and divine protection through legal testament, and the Jewish people, at Sinai, was given the Torah as "the user's guide" for managing the conditional premises of its *people-wide* observance or neglect. From our very beginnings, truth, justice and the welfare of what we call society are seen in the corporate condition of the people — credits for performance and the penalties for ignoring Torah were always understood in terms of group consequentiality — salvation has always been *national* salvation; effect has always been *corporate* effect and meaning has always been aggregate meaning. The individual Jew will enjoy salvation because the Jewish people has been redeemed; the individual Jew will enjoy immortality because the nation of Israel is immortal; the individual is worthy because our people is worthy and in whatever the individual is deficient, the merit of the Family sustains.

---

[12] A collection of Rabbinic homilies, narrative, didactics and commentary on the biblical book of Leviticus, compiled between the 1st and 5th centuries CE.

The sanctity of group; the holiness of the plenum; the virtue of combined endeavor — for Jews these have always been leading characteristics of meaning and purpose. An individual's joy is our collective joy; personal tragedy is the pain of the many. For centuries, the Jewish utterance in the presence of mourners has been "May God comfort *you* among *all* those who mourn for Zion and Jerusalem." It is remarkable that Jewish tradition instructs that, upon the death of an individual for whom no family mourners remain, unrelated members of the Jewish community are obligated to sit in the house of mourning and receive consoling visitors. The concept of *minyan* (the quorum of ten needed for the exercise of particular ritual functions) likewise, is after all, the concept of community in action (and maybe even the origin of the concept of "group coverage"). We laugh, we cry, we pray, we study, we work, we celebrate, we believe, we doubt, we dream, we build . . . personally, to be sure, but, in the final analysis, the self acquires its fullest meaning and its most determinative shaping in community.

"I FOUND IT!" Remember the bumper stickers a few years ago, promoted as part of Christian religious revival? One Jewish wag proposed that our appropriate response (if indeed, any response at all was needed) would be "WE NEVER LOST IT!" Harvard Divinity School Theologian Rev. Dr. Harvey Cox correctly observed: ". . . This says something important to us about the faith of Israel: it is not the faith of individuals but the faith of a people."[13] Much more can be said about the "IT" but the "WE" rings loud and clear.

2.

Not with you alone do I make this covenant with its sanctions but even with those...who are not here with us today — 'Even with all the future generations.' (Rashi, on Deuteronomy 29:1314)[14]

---

[13] *Many Mansions: A Christian's Encounter With Other Faiths*, Beacon Press, 1988.

[14] Rashi, the acronym for (Ra)bbi (Sh)lomo (I)tzhaqi, 1040-1105, French-German teacher, scholar, biblical and Talmudic commentator, legal decisor; widely considered to be one of the most outstanding and influential sages of all Jewish history. See also Babylonian Talmud, *Shevuot* 39a.

I was at Sinai, you were at Sinai...we were *all* at Sinai, even those of us who don't remember and even those who joined the Family later. We were all witnesses to a great and indescribable event. We may not be able to recount the details but we *do* know we heard God speak and that we received the Torah. It had been a long, hard journey from those days when we shared our tents with Abraham and Sarah, from crowding around the tables with Jacob, Rachel and Leah. We suffered plenty in the cauldron of Egyptian oppression but, with God's help, we left the "House of Bondage," reached Sinai, stayed a while and were never the same again. We built a nation, we built a Temple and we built a society the others never even conceived of. I have a history, you have a history . . . all Jews have a history — we belonged even before we got here and we will belong even after we're gone.

3.

"...if you would know a people, would know what motivates them, would know what they really care about, study their rituals. Rituals...reveal the convictions a society has about life." (John E. Burkhart)-15

When was the last time you touched your children and looked deeply into their eyes (especially after they became teenagers)? When of late have you had the pleasure of transforming your living space into an oasis of beauty and tranquility? Do you recall the last time, with no ulterior motives, you told your spouse you loved her? How about those occasions on which you helped the unfortunate *without* being asked? How does simple food become a banquet and when did you last celebrate just how well off you really are (and without telling anyone)? Jews can answer these questions because Jews celebrate rituals and Jewish rituals are the roadways to all these things.

---

15 *Worship*, Westminster Press, 1982, p.24.

4.

> When you make a loan of any kind to your neigh-
> bor, do not go into his house to reclaim his collater-
> al. Stand outside and let the man to whom you are
> making the loan bring the collateral out to you. If
> the man is poor, do not go to sleep with his pledge
> in your possession. Return his collateral to him by
> sunset so that he may sleep with his pledged gar-
> ment. Then he will thank you, and it will be
> regarded as a righteous act in the sight of the Lord
> your God. (*Deuteronomy* 24:10-13)

Jews were not the first to set laws against murder, rape, false testimony, adultery and theft. Jews *were* the first to raise the value of human life to the ultimate level ("image of God") and, consequently, *were* the first to remove theft of property from the category of capital crime (ponder that a bit as you read the daily newspaper). Jews were not the first to devise rules of evidence, but Jews *were* the first to reject the validity of circumstantial evidence in capital cases (ponder that one too, in the same daily newspaper). Jews were not the first to design loans or instruments of capital or concepts of interest, but Jews *were* the first to insist that a lender's right to collateral does not include violation of the borrower's dignity ("stand outside") and that lending money to a person in need is a Godly act.

Jews did not invent credit cards (even like the kind you get in the mail without asking) but Jews *were* the first to prohibit the encouraging of another person to live beyond his means. Jews did not originate meaning but Jews *were* the first to teach that *every-thing* people do is consequential. Jews did not invent labor contracts but Jews *were* the first to obligate the employer to provide worktime meals at his own expense. Jews did not invent involvement but Jews *were* the first to prohibit "standing idly by" while another person suffers. Jews did not invent law codes but Jews *were* the first to require that The Law be read periodically, to the entire public, and in a language they would understand (even if they didn't finish high school). Jews did not invent weights and measures but Jews *were* the first to insist that merchants tip the scales in favor of the buyer (and that measuring devices be adjusted periodically to compensate for temperature and humidity.) Jews were not the first to discover love, but Jews *were* the first to insist that it's not what you *say* but what you *do* that counts. *First*, and *still* at it...without much competition.

5.

"The World To Be . . . does exist." (Maimonides)[16]

It is significant that the Torah begins by portraying the creation of an ideal world (Genesis 1:1-2:4, for convenience, we'll call it The Seven Days). Everything following the opening depiction is, in some way, inferior to what is described in the Bible's opening verses. How is it these few hundred words remain part of biblical narrative which spans twenty-four (or 39, depending on how you count) books and is comprised of many thousands of words? The answer is that the Torah's opening portrait is a depiction not of what *is* but of what *can* be. The narrative reflects, for Jewish and non-Jewish reader alike (as this is a *universal* story, not a Jewish one), a condition, a set of circumstances of which we get only glimpses in our own lives.

The Adam and Eve story (*Genesis* 2:4-3:24) looks much more like the world we know: male-centeredness, violation of limits, passing the buck, discord among humans, the natural world and God, punishment, mortality, pain and exile. What's The Seven Days got to do with all the rest of Bible and reality? The Seven Days is indeed the portrayal of a world we do not know but, at the same time, it is the portrayal of a world which Jews believe can be achieved.

The Torah does not begin with the story of the Jewish people, it does not begin with a claim to the Land of Israel. The Torah does not begin with covenant or law or tribe or festival or

---

[16] *Mishneh Torah, Laws of Repentence*, 8:8. Moses ben Maimon, 1135-1204, philosopher, rabbi, jurist, physician. His writings have had more influence upon Judaism than any single individual since the first Moses.

ritual or particularity — the Torah opens with an astonishing portrayal of *all humanity's* world, of a reality beyond gender and race and ethnos and religion. In the Torah's initial picture, there is represented a world brought into being by a benevolent Creator-God, a world of goodness ("and it was good"), a world of dependability ("and it was so"), a world of harmoniousness where all the component elements are interdependent and interrelated. Male and female humanity is exquisitely equal (no ribs here) and God-like in its dimensions ("in the image of God"), living in a fertile, abundant environment of concord and benign human management. The world of The Seven Days has no conflict, no hatred, no factionalism. The world of The Seven Days has no politics and no religion. The world of The Seven Days has a single father/mother for the entire human race and the world of The Seven Days has no territorial boundaries and no fences and no armies and no hunger and no death. All the rest of Bible and Jewish history (and everyone's history) is less than the picture of The Seven Days but, then again, The Seven Days is not what *is,* rather what isn't . . . *yet.* How do we get there? The Torah shows us The Seven Days' perfected world because all the rest of Torah and Jewish tradition will be the program for getting there. No universal ideal can be accomplished without a particular program. We're still working on ours.

6.

"It seems to be the role of the Jews to focus and
dramatize the common experiences of mankind, and
to turn their particular fate into a universal moral.
They always knew that Jewish society was appointed to be a pilot-project for the entire human race."
(Paul Johnson)[17]

To speak the truth and be abhorred for doing so. To "keep your head when all about you are losing theirs and blaming it on you." To find in even the lowliest of us a universe of possibility.

---

[17] *A History of the Jews,* Harper & Row, 1987, p.586.

To be pushed and shoved through the pages of history and still believe in yourself. To look at all the same things everyone else has looked at for ages and yet see something more. To be held to the sides and then discover the creativity that comes of being marginal. To be marginal and central at the same time. To contend that their certainties are open to question and that verity comes in plural forms. To insist that our truths are not everyone's truths and that you don't have to be Jewish to be a mensch. To see God and Godliness in all creation and yet remember that visual acuity is variable. To know that there just might be a better way to do it even if they say there isn't. To say "Why not?" when they tell you it can't be done. To have experienced some of the most bestial in our fellow creatures and still affirm life. To take a good, hard look at where you've been and how far you've come and what remains to be done and say "Thank you, God!"

ABORTION — ETHICAL IS NOT ALWAYS JEWISH

As in so many things, we Jews are often our own worst enemies. Unfortunately, it seems we have frequent occasion to see this truth boldly represented. These days, the abortion rights controversy swirls about our heads; state legislatures are beginning to vie with one another as to which can rush to restrictive legislation first. Newspapers and television continue to predict the reversal of Rowe v. Wade and those of us on the receiving end of regressive and oppressive law are growing more uncomfortable.

For those who take Jewish affairs seriously and who endeavor to view and understand national and world affairs through the filter of our tradition, the abortion controversy is laden with significance. We are in a position to make enormous contributions to the debate and, by and large, we have been dropping the ball. First off, it must be said that we have to resist, with all our resources, the semantic tyranny of current labels. If we use the phrase "Pro Life" as a label for anti-abortion groups, and we allow its use to go unchecked and unchallenged, then the label "Pro Choice" for those favoring abortion rights becomes equivalent to "Pro Death"!! As Jews, we can and should be unflinchingly "Pro Life" (the undeniable bias of the entirety of our tradition, from Torah on) and still maintain the position that abortion, in defined instances, is affirmative of that value.

Many of our people have been caught up with the slogan "We control our own bodies" as a leading contention in the position regarding abortion rights. The fact is, however, that the phrase is *not* a Jewish one despite the fact, once again, that many Jews use it! Judaism regards the relationship of body to person as *stewardship* of that which has been given by The Creator in trust; there are ample attestations in our tradition of obligations to maintain the body (legislation concerning tattooing, incising, wounding, healing, cleansing, burying, etc.) and, in no way can it be said that the individual is the ultimate arbiter of what can and cannot be done with the physical container of our being.

The problem is that many Jews have confused their liberal social/political commitments with Jewish values, assuming all too glibly that the best of this liberalism and the best of Judaism are synonymous. Sometimes, that is gloriously true. Other times, our liberal ideals are in conflict with Jewish ideals and knowledge and sensitivity and care are much needed to tell the difference. All the while we take a liberal *political/social* position regarding abortion rights, we undermine the fundamental Jewish *religious* position which, upon examination is much more cogent and much more validating. To allow our position on abortion rights to be presented as a political stance exposes us to all the risks which define the *political* world — a position can be outvoted, a position can be bought or sold, a position can be overridden or "influenced" or negotiated away. To take a *political* position on abortion rights is to render abortion rights vulnerable to political management.

The Jewish tradition (from *Exodus* 21:22 on) does not consider abortion to be murder. Judaism considers the fetus to be an appendage of the mother[18] and the welfare of the mother to be PRIOR to the welfare of the fetus. The Jewish tradition considers rape, incest, physical anguish and mental anguish to be reasonable indications for abortion.[19] Indeed, in defined circumstances, Judaism considers abortion a *mitzvah!*

The world around us speaks of the immorality of abortion, and as we are witnessing almost daily, appeals to morals and ethics seem to infuse all the restrictive arguments. For four years the Federal government extended the ban on Federal financing of research using transplanted fetal tissue. Despite the claims of legions of researchers that such investigation holds significant

---

[18] *Babylonian Talmud, Hullin* 58a; *Gittin* 32b, etc.

[19] See Rabbi David M. Feldman's superb *Marital Relations, Birth Control And Abortion In Jewish Law,* Schocken Books, 1974, especially pp.268ff.)

promise for the alleviation of such maladies as juvenile diabetes and Parkinson's disease, government spokesmen appealed to the "immorality" of such research.   Dr. James O. Mason who announced the continuation of the government ban in 1989 said that ". . . the decision to extend the ban was a matter of heart and of mind as well."   Mason argued that the research pits the rights of fetuses against those of patients who would be helped, so he felt obliged to come down on the side of the fetuses.   Dr. John C. Willke, president of the National Right to Life Committee (note the semantics!) also argued that the issue "is not one of politics versus science, but rather what manner of *ethical* (my emphasis) constraints will govern federally funded research . . . by electing an Administration pledged to oppose abortion, American society had determined that certain types of research are *unethical* (my emphasis), no matter how useful the data they produce."   Ethics by vote!?   *Then,* indeed, unethics by outvoting!!   And what about the fact that where we're coming from, many Rabbinic authorities would consider fetal tissue research to be the *highest* purpose to which such tissue could be put!

For us the matter is neither one of ethics nor of politics; our tradition provides for abortion in the context of our religious values and our supreme regard for the sanctity of life.   People like Mason or Willke cannot speak for our religious values and principles.   For us, fetal tissue holds the promise of enhancing life and alleviating the suffering of untold millions; for us, the dictates of our Torah and our tradition hold the paramount importance in defining and mitigating our acts.   Our taking an abortion rights position through Judaism can only safeguard our rights and enhance our tradition.   We owe it to who and what we are to present our postures to the world around us as indeed our *religious* principles, *principles no less potent and no less valid* than the understandings at which the Christian world has arrived.

Our rejection of restrictive abortion legislation comes from the free and unfettered practice of Judaism and we must oppose every manifestation of the intrusion of the state into religion.   We should reaffirm our religious and cultural integrity in a society predicated upon democratic religious pluralism.   As Americans and as Jews we embrace the Constitution, as Americans and as Jews we embrace the Bill of Rights and, true to ourselves, as Americans and Jews we embrace the right to Torah as our guide.

MORAL EQUATIONISM

Some time ago, Karl E. Meyer of the *New York Times* wrote of the paradoxical fact that Theodor Herzl was inspired by the music of Richard Wagner, the very composer whose work, for many years now, the Israel Philharmonic has refused to perform. Wagner, of course, a virulent anti-semite on his own accord, was a favorite of Adolf Hitler for whom Wagner's music embodied the vitality, promise and triumphal superiority of the Third Reich. Quoting Amos Elon's biography of Herzl, Meyer informed us that ". . . for inspiration and to dispel occasional doubts, Herzl turned to Wagnerian music. He was enraptured by the music of the great anti-Semite . . . and faithfully attended every performance of Wagner at the Paris Opera." "For Herzl," says Meyer, "'Tannhauser' inspired visions of liberation that mattered far more than the Jew-baiting of its composer." Meyer then leaped to the conclusive points that ". . . all great works of art take on an existence independent of their creators' prejudices. For a free society to bar public performances of Wagner finds an unseemly parallel in Nazi bans on performing Mendelssohn because he was Jewish."

There it is, staring one in the face . . . another painful example of the fuzzy thinking and perverse pseudo-logic which irresponsible newspapers and editors allow to pass for journalism and contributions to public enlightenment! Once more, in slightly altered garb, is the morally relativistic equation of Jews and their behaviors with the depraved acts of their detractors. The insidious suggestion that bans on Mendelssohn and Wagner are parallel is all but horrifying! How could a person simply ignore the fact that Mendelssohn was the VICTIM in the ban of his music and that Wagner was a PERPETRATOR? How could anyone fail to see that Wagner was an active proponent of racial hatred and social exclusionism while Felix Mendelssohn exhibited not even a whisper of the same during his entire lifetime?! And more.

While Herzl may have been enamored of Wagner it must also be said that Herzl did not live quite long enough to hear Wagner played by concentration camp orchestras welcoming new arrivals to Hell nor did Herzl enjoy the merit of witnessing Wagner's greatest aficionado, against the background of his music, call for the conquest of the world and the elimination of all its Jews!   To suggest that there might be even the slightest parallel between Nazi bans on Mendelssohn and an Israel Philharmonic ban on Wagner is to take rank with the vilest perversions of logic. And such parallel striking is familiar to us as a recurring manifestation of the attempt to either delegitimize the Jewish state or impugn the tradition of Jewish morality through such claims as the Nazi-like treatment of Palestinians by the Israeli government (if Israel treated the Palestinians as Nazis, there would not *be* a Palestinian problem!!). Moral equationism has become one of the most potent weapons of contemporary Jew-haters and Jew-baiters; its effectiveness, sadly, is proportional to the mass of the population of sloppy thinkers and half-educated unsophisticates produced, at least in our own country, by educational institutions which have ceased teaching how to read and how to think.

I reject the notion that art "takes on an existence independent of their creators' prejudices." Artistic expression, to me, is the *fullness* of the associations and allusions of the creation. The artistic experience is the experience of the totality of the creation; its richness and impact are the combined total of all that the creation is and all that its creator has brought to bear, consciously and unconsciously, to the work he has produced. I cannot appreciate the bas reliefs of Temple destruction portrayed on the Arch of Titus. I cannot revel in the artistic beauty of Medieval carvings depicting Sinagoga as vanquished by Church Triumphant. I am not uplifted by the supposed artistic excellence of the portraiture of Ferdinand and Isabella hanging in the Prado.

Indeed, precisely because the artistic experience, at best, should evoke *all* that both creator and viewer bring to it, I am not willing (and perhaps, in truth, not able) to separate the fullness of my consciousness and my values from the supposed virtue of *ars gratia artis*. And I say this even at the risk that moral equationists will equate me with the Philistines!

KOSHER HAS NOTHING TO DO
WITH FOOD

I suppose most people who ever think about it believe that kosher has everything in the world to do with food. Honestly, I can't blame people for thinking this. After all, kosher does have to do with dairy foods and meat foods and things you can't eat and things you can. It has to do with which forks can be used with which knives and which plates can hold what edibles. Just about everybody knows that pork isn't kosher (not so sure about lobster tails) and just about everybody knows that Orthodox rabbis usually don't eat anywhere but home. Many people have colorful reminiscences of grandmothers (called bubbas in those days) who would sooner die than mix dairy tableware with meat tableware, grandmothers who were certain that any violation of the kosher "laws" would probably bring immediate divine wrath. Many Jews also remember when, despite being raised in a kosher home, they ate their first bacon somewhere else and. . . wonder of wonders . . . didn't drop dead. For many of those people, the only thing that died was their continuing the practice of "keeping kosher" (=kashrut). For some, serving in the U.S. Army did it, for others, going away to school brought kashrut to an end. Yet others, born of intellectually liberated Socialist parents, never had kashrut to do away with and still others, desirous of being truly American, discarded this outdated leftover of Eastern European Jewish superstition and unenlightenment.

Let's take a brief look at some of what kashrut is in the Torah and Jewish tradition. In the main, these points really stand out (I am ignoring many other important details in order to maximize focus here):

- •eating the meat and milk only of quadruped, split-hoofed, cud-chewing mammals (no horses, for example)
- •eating no carrion (e.g. no road kill)
- •eating no pork (no matter how good those ribs smell)
- •eating fish only with both scales and fins (shrimp are out)
- •eating only the fowl enumerated in the Torah and in tradition; no carrion-consumers and no predators (no condor cutlets and certainly no barbecued eagle wings)
- •eating no blood of anything (blutwurst is a no-no)
- •eating no insects, except for a few locust species (eeecchh)
- •not cooking or mixing milk and meat together (bye, bye cheeseburgers).

This certainly makes it look like we're talking about eating, doesn't it? Well, we're not done yet, we've only just begun.

For many years, many people, Jews and non-Jews alike, have been convinced that basically, the laws of kashrut were laid down for health reasons. In particular, people point out, the prohibition against pork was instituted to protect against trichinosis, still a health problem in many parts of the world. Now, it is argued, with things like government inspection, refrigeration and scientific knowledge, such prohibitions are no longer necessary. The response I have been offering my students for years in this regard is: if the kashrut laws were intended for health reasons then, over the long haul of time, the Gentiles should have died out and the world's population should be primarily kashrut-observing Jewish! The Chinese have been ignoring kashrut for millennia and look how they're doing (maybe that's why so many Jews like to eat Chinese food?).

If the "health rationale" for kashrut doesn't work, then we'll have to look elsewhere. Perhaps we should think about food taboos. Throughout the world, we are able to observe very many traditions as to what can and cannot be eaten. These traditions in many ways have become national characteristics. Consider for instance that in Southeast Asia, dog meat is a well-regarded human food source and consider how repulsive the thought of eating poodle patties sounds to the Western sensitivity! But, consider also, the many virtues of dog meat (high quality protein, low fat, inexpensive, easily raised, etc.) and the fact that, *inherently*, the consumption of dog meat is no worse than eating beef or lamb. The whole matter has more to do with cultural conditioning than anything else — not health, not wholesomeness, not taste — cultural conditioning. And so it is around the world.

There can be no doubt that some significant part of Jewish dietary tradition must be understood in the context of cultural conditioning; there is no reason to believe that only Jews, among the peoples of the world, have been free of this anthropological fact. Something else seems to be operating in the Jewish sphere.

A careful examination of the kashrut regulations reveals a different dynamic at work, a dynamic that has more to do with particularity than with protein. A theme which appears throughout our ancient literature, starting with the Torah, is the theme of our differentness. Very early on, we recognized that our culture was constantly under the threat of being overcome by the more powerful, more influential peoples around us. We understood well that there were concepts, ideas, values and truths to which we held and which were often at great variance with our neighbors. It was these very variances which comprised the definition of who we were, whether we were speaking of the idea of God or the concept of the sublime nature and holiness of the human being — we understood from the very start that the things which, for us, were undeniable truths were, for others, either wrong, threatening, offensive or meaningless. If we were desirous of preserving, of holding on to our peculiarities of vision and meaning, then steps would have to be taken to protect against the disintegration of our uniqueness in an undifferentiating world.

Basically put, the question was: What can we do to assure that what is dear to us not be overwhelmed and disappear? We always knew we were a small people and we always knew that we were at risk of being culturally flattened by the steam roller of history. We always knew that we were more important to ourselves than to anybody else. We always knew that our moral and ethical values were worthy and just and that, more than anything else, we had to make sure that they wouldn't vanish.

That's where we began to identify those aspects of our mundane existence which might serve to maintain and convey the very non-mundane things we were thinking about. We hit upon the notion that sustaining a sense of our differentness would be a powerful tool for holding on to the *substance* of that differentness and that the preservation of uniqueness had to be a steady, constant, ongoing phenomenon. We hit upon the idea of attaching identity markers to many of the varied and sundry aspects of our day-to-day living. That meant, in a certain sense, employing devices which, while in and of themselves were not significant, would nonetheless make convenient markers for values and purposes which indeed were. In Jewish civilization there are literally hundreds of such markers/hooks. They are associated with virtually all facets of our daily lives — dress, prayer, grooming, language, personal hygiene, ritual and . . . food. In each of these areas, there are practices and conventions which exist solely for the purpose of highlighting the uniqueness of the practitioners, believing, as we do, that accenting uniqueness is one of the most effective possible steps in preserving what that uniqueness *is all about.* We have always understood that these markers are only *markers* and that it would be foolish and erroneous to ascribe substantive meaning to something which is only a means to an end and surely not an end in itself. This is the key for understanding kashrut and an examination of even a few examples will drive the point home clearly.

We consider a meal to be a religious act, an act which calls to mind our relationship with the world around us and our dependence upon the benevolence of the Source of all nourishment. A meal is more than the ingestion of nutrition — everyone eats, everyone must eat but *how* we eat differentiates us from the rest of nature and from those who invest eating with meanings (or non-meanings) different from ours.

Milk and meat are separated because milk and meat represent two distinct realms of reality. Milk represents life and nurture and meat represents death and finality. Jews believe it is important to remind ourselves constantly of the existence of multiple realms, to maintain our ability to see the component uniqueness of creation and to appreciate the elements of the various facets of reality. Jews reject a homogenized view of reality, arguing that the mission to make the world better, to enhance the human condition, requires that we have a clear view of that very world, the humanity we are pledged to engage. Surely, our world is an immensely complex and wonderful fabric of harmonious interrelations but also, at the same time, it is a unity of diverse and individuated parts. Those parts, those differentiated elements (like individual people) have worth, have integrity, have their own meaning and value, have been created by their Creator to be such. Therefore, we do well to bring ourselves, as often as possible, to see and to appreciate the parts of the whole. Eating, like so many of the things we do in life, involves destruction and such destruction, for the eater, means life. Milk is life and meat is death and our separating these two realms enables us to see, ever more clearly, that the most commonplace acts are filled with significance. Jews are forbidden to eat blood because blood is a symbol of life. We embrace the paradox of killing an animal for food, but we do it in such a way as to not take its "life."[20] Jews have a tradition of ritual slaughter (*shehitah*) because, in killing an animal for food we do not want to lose our compassion for life.[21]

> We do not eat predators because we do not want to identify with predation.[22]
> We do not eat carrion because we have not been able to perform *shehitah*.
> We don't eat pork because they *do* and we separate milk and meat because they *don't*.

Ideas, to become real and dynamic, need traction. Values, concepts, appreciations, vision need instrumentalities through which they can become kinetic and thus, can be made to happen. Kashrut is a vehicle for sensitizing ourselves to the holiness that can be

---

[20] See *Leviticus* 17:11-14 - "For the life of the flesh is in the blood...No person among you shall eat blood...If any Israelite or stranger who lives among them should hunt down an animal or a bird that may be eaten, he shall pour out its blood and cover it with earth for the life of all flesh--its blood is its life... .

[21] *Shehitah* requires that an animal be slaughtered by a pious and gentle *human being* who must be in *physical contact* with the animal he is killing.

[22] "The ox is pursued by the lion, the lamb is pursued by the wolf, the goat is pursued by the leopard - therefore, the Holy One, Blessed be He said: "Do not offer before Me any pursuer, rather [offer for sacrifice] those who are pursued...always should a person be like the pursued...like the dove...and not like the pursuer." *Vayikra Rabbah* (Margoliot), parashah 27; *Otzar Hamidrashim,* (Eisenstein), 270:4.

brought to the commonplace. Kashrut is a means for inculcating in ourselves and in our children a sense of yes and no, of "you may" and "you may not." Kashrut speaks to us of the value of limit. Kashrut reminds us that human benefit comes through loss. Kashrut reminds us "I'm more than just an animal, I'm a human." Kashrut reminds us "I'm more than just a human, I'm a Jew!"[23]

---

[23] Rabbi Eleazar ben Azariah said: '...a person should not say..."I do not wish to eat pork or I do not wish to commit adultery" but rather "I would indeed like to do these things but what can I do, God has forbidden me." That is why the Torah says "I (God) have differentiated you from the other nations to be Mine" (*Leviticus* 20:26) - For thus shall a person separate himself from wrongdoing and do God's will.' [Sifra, *Kedoshim* 9:9] *Sifra,* sometimes called *Torat Kohanim* is a 1st century CE collection of Rabbinic commentary on the book of *Leviticus.*

OF MEN AND SUPERMEN

Like many of you, I was brought up with Superman and Clark Kent and I still have vivid childhood recollections of the adventures of the man of steel. I remember anxiously waiting for the next comic book to arrive at the newsstand and how, at 5:30 PM, radio time was set aside for Jorel's son. So, what's Superman got to do with the Jewish question? In my earlier years, I don't think I even would have understood the question, but now, as wisdom and maturity set in, I fear I understand all too well what Superman means in American hero iconography and how very, very much significant Jewish interests are actually and potentially affected.

I have made the point in the past that the widespread overglorification and IDEALIZATION of the heroic model in western civilization (Mother Teresa, Dr. Albert Schweitzer) stands in the way of many people's ability to see Oskar Schindler as a true hero, that with all his faults and flaws and his never resolved base character, he saved lives, the highest virtue to which one can aspire. I argued as I would argue again that idealized models of heroism, deeply influenced by Christian tradition, preclude the likelihood that many of us common, regular, ordinary folks would, in a future tragedy, rise to the occasion because of our conditioned view of our unworthiness. If all that makes sense, then take another look at Superman!

Let's consider just nine, count 'em, nine characteristics of Superman, which are prominent in the persona he projects and then contemplate what the accumulating message is all about, what it says about OUR ability to achieve heroism.

1. Superman is not of this world. He lives among us for sure, but his home was in Krypton, some unknown part of the solar system . . . he is not earthly in his origin nor in his qualities. In a word, he is among us but not OF US.

2. Superman has x-ray vision, nothing is closed to his extraterrestrial piercing stare. Superman has visual powers unknown to any earthling (that's us) . . . Superman has astounding sight but Superman has no INSIGHT! No portrayal of Superman that I have ever encountered portrays him as contemplative or introspective. It is only in the most basic sense that Superman sees and when something has to be looked into, it is the fabled x-ray vision he employs as a substitute for thinking.

3. Superman is never wrong! You will search in vain to discover even one instance in which the superhero ever admits to error, to misjudgment or misapprehension. He never has to apologize, he never offends, he never takes a misstep. He never has to clean up after he's done.

4. Superman indeed is the Man of Steel. With his extraordinary (think about that word!) power, he can leap buildings in a single bound and uproot mountains with a single hand. Superman is the epitome of strength and brute force with which he destroys evil and sets matters aright but never will you find him using powers of mediation or moral suasion to confront conflict and achieve resolution. Superman's power is in his muscle but not in his mentality!

5. Superman is solitary, his relationships are superficial and perhaps even artificial. As a recent movie portrayed it, his getaway is somewhere in the arctic, in a crystal palace of enormous dimension in which he is the only occupant. Superman doesn't really live anywhere, he has no neighbors even when he's in town, in fact he hangs out a lot in telephone booths.

6. Superman is passionless. He doesn't eat, he doesn't drink, he doesn't blow his cool. Superman, after all these decades, still hasn't "made it" with Lois Lane who, incidentally, is the only source of his awkwardness and lack of ease. The great hero doesn't really have time for women or most other good things, come to think of it.

7. Superman's only weakness is external. In the presence of kryptonite, the mineral of which his home planet was composed, Superman loses his phenomenal powers and weakens to the point of near death. Unlike us ordinary human beings afflicted with doubt, inner turmoil, hangups, disease and turmoil,

his only nemesis is outside himself, never within.

8. Superman is ageless. Oh, of course, Superboy was around for a while as the comic books attempted to develop an additional market but, in fact, aside from this brief appearance, Superman has remained unchanged throughout the decades. How utterly wonderful — he entered adult life without ever having had to be an adolescent!

9. Superman spends most of his time masquerading as someone else. It is a token of the superficiality of his relationships that those around him (going on fifty years now!!) haven't yet figured out who Clark Kent really is and all the time they spend with him is time spent with someone other than whom they think he is. Unless he is wearing his beautiful blue spandex uniform which covers a flawless male body, nobody knows him for what he is.

What might we imagine are the subtle and cumulative effects of this heroic model on the American psyche? No desire to get overly dramatic here but...what do our hero images say about ourselves? Superman's qualities are *not* our qualities and Superman's reality is *not* our reality. Surely, Superman is nowhere near what we call an accessible model and surely Superman contributes to that ever-growing sense that we mere mortals are not and cannot be heroes! Here in the popular imagination, once again, is an image with which we cannot identify, who teaches us in the most subtle and subliminal ways that the truly heroic things people do are not worthy.

How about quiet acts of *tzedakah,* or what about raising Jewish children in an alien environment? How about extricating Jews from lands of oppression and suffering? What about the loyal and loving care of sons and daughters for their elderly and infirm parents and the struggle of so many to make a good life for their families? What about all the unspoken kindnesses and sacrifices and devotions made so often at great personal cost? Come to think of it, we are surrounded by Supermen and Superwomen in the very mundaneness of our daily lives, super people whose quiet humanity and fragility and vulnerability and love of Torah make life a blessing.

"JUSTICE, JUSTICE SHALL YOU PURSUE"

Readers will easily recognize that one of the recurring themes in these pages is the enormous actual and potential contributions Judaism has made and can yet make to civilization (once Jews finally learn what we're all about!). Jewish values, perceptions and concepts relate to every sphere of human endeavor and concern. Some sense of what we mean by *tiqqun olam* is that the unique richness of our tradition, through us, contributes, in some way, to making the world better. In the realm of jurisprudence we can see some of the most compelling aspects of Judaism's conception of "the way things ought to be." And it is this area that deserves our attention currently. Can there be any doubt that we are in the midst of a public crisis of confidence with respect to our justice system. Pennsylvania, in 1995, impeached and unseated one of its Supreme Court judges. The character of Supreme Court Justice Clarence Thomas is revisited from time to time. Continuing tales of bribery, sinister influence and unbecoming behavior fill our newspapers, magazines and books. Commerce Secretary Espy, it seems, couldn't tell the difference between chicken and chicanery. Senator Robert Packwood protected himself from the long arm of the law by hiding behind the protective veil of a Senate "Ethics Committee" (what does "ethics" mean?). For Judaism, contemporary events and eroded public regard for law constitute a nightmare come true. What is society if not the fragile compact created by shared confidence in the machinery of law and justice?

A serious look at our jurisprudential tradition can be most instructive. I harbor no notion that America will be converted to Torah but I do believe strongly that a clear portrayal of some of the essence of what we stand for can be quite compelling and attractive for people who think and who care.

As is so often the case, reference to the masterwork of Moses Ben Maimon, the *Mishneh Torah,* can be quite instructive. Before looking at Maimonides, however, a few clarifications are in order. Jewish law (*halakhah*) does not provide either for juries or for lawyers. Cases (criminal and civil) are tried before judicial panels ranging in size from three jurists to seventy-one (the Great Sanhedrin).

Individuals can be consulted by the court and the litigant/defendant for advice but, in the usual state of affairs, litigants and defendants present their own cases before the judicial panel which ultimately renders the decision in the matter. Consequently, Jewish classical texts will speak unvaryingly about *judges* but, in our contemporary context, these texts are speaking also about legislators, lawmakers and public officials with any connection to the management and application of law.

What of qualifications for service? Who should be a judge and what characteristics should such individuals possess? Commanding public presence is considered a positive value because it encourages confidence in the system. Wide knowledge of many subjects increases the chances that the jurist will understand the matters and the people who come before him. Being conversant with the language of the litigants reduces the chance for translation errors of fact or nuance:

> Only those are eligible to serve as members of the Sanhedrin . . . who are wise men and understanding, that is, who are experts in the Torah and versed in many other branches of learning; who possess some knowledge of the general sciences such as medicine, mathematics, the calculation of cycles and constellations; and are somewhat acquainted with astrology, the arts of diviners, soothsayers, sorcerers, the superstitious practices of idolaters, and similar matters, so that they be competent to deal with cases requiring such knowledge...Every conceivable effort should be made to the end that all the members of the tribunal be of mature age, imposing stature, good appearance, and that they be able to express their views in clear and well-chosen words, and be

conversant with most of the spoken languages, in order that the Sanhedrin may dispense with the services of an interpreter. [Maimonides, *Mishneh Torah, Judges*[24], 21:6]

The notion of the jurist's comprehension of the litigant's assertions is so highly regarded that again, Maimonides states the obligation to limit recourse to an interpreter —

The judge shall not hear the arguments from the mouth of an interpreter unless he knows the language spoken by the litigants and understands their arguments. If he is unable to speak their language fluently enough to address them, he may appoint an interpreter to advise them of the decision to set forth the reason for pronouncing one guilty and the other innocent. [21:8]

The wonderful complexity of human nature is well-recognized by Jewish jurisprudence. Anyone familiar with the inside (and outside) stories of personality clashes among jurists (yes, even in our highest courts!) will appreciate the rule that:

Two scholars who dislike each other are forbidden to sit together in judgement, for this might lead to the rendering of a perverted judgement. Prompted by hostility, each will be inclined to refute the arguments of the other. [23:7]

From the very beginning we seem to have preferred leaders who shunned the very office to which they were appointed. Moses tried, unsuccessfully, on a number of occasions to avoid appointment, to no avail. And ever since Moses, we have honored reluctance as a becoming characteristic (what does it mean to "run" for office?) and it should come as no surprise to read —

. . . He who shuns the office of judge avoids enmity, robbery and false swearing. . . . [20:8]

---

[24] All subsequent references are from this source, translation by Isadore Twersky, *A Maimonides Reader*, Behrman, 1972.

Of course, people are innocent until *proven* guilty but the mental attitude of the judge is quite significant. As a check against judicial bias, Judaism, even long before Maimonides urged that —

> At all times while the litigants are before you regard them as guilty, on the presumption that there is no truth in the statements made by either of them, and be guided by what appears to you from the general drift of the arguments to be true. But when they have departed from your presence, regard them both as innocent, since they have acquiesced in the sentence passed by you, and judge each of them by the scale of merit. [23:10]

The mental attitude of the judge is a major consideration in Jewish tradition and extraordinary steps are taken to assure, as much as possible, that bias and prejudicial thinking do not intrude. Maimonides addresses mental attitude in a most remarkable way —

> Whence do we derive that the judge who has reason to suspect one of the litigants of misrepresentation should not say "I will decide the case according to the evidence and let the witnesses bear the responsibility"? Because it is said: "Keep far from a false matter" (*Exodus* 23:7). How is he to proceed in such a case? Let him sedulously investigate the witnesses with the inquiries and queries to which witnesses in capital cases are subjected. If, after this thoroughgoing examination, he concludes [that there is nothing fraudulent about the suit, he gives his decision on the basis of the evidence. But if he has any scruples about it], suspecting dishonesty, or has no confidence in the witnesses, although he has no valid ground on which to disqualify them, or he is inclined to believe that the litigant is a subtle fraud, that the witnesses are honest men, giving their evidence in all innocence, but were led astray by the litigant, or it appears to him from the whole tenor of the proceedings that some information is withheld,

or brought into the open — in any of these or similar circumstances *the judge is forbidden to render a decision.* He should withdraw from the case and let another judge, who can without qualms of conscience pronounce judgement, handle it . . . [24:3]

The discretionary power of the judge is enormous, not only in the Jewish system but surely in the American system as well. It is this very discretionary element which should cause us all great concern, for the subjectivity of discretion reflects the character and quality of the decisor. Who is he, what does he believe? What are his views about people and things? What are his religious biases and what about his political leanings? We know that people bring all that they are to bear upon the things they do and say and the discretionary powers of the judge challenge the very foundations of justice itself —

. . . discretionary power is vested in the judge. He is to decide whether the offender deserves these punishments and whether the emergency of the hour demands their application. But whatever the expedient he sees fit to resort to, all his deeds should be done for the sake of heaven. [24:10]

Let not human dignity be light in his eyes; for the respect due to man supersedes a negative rabbinical command...The judge must be careful not to do anything calculated to destroy his *self-respect.* [*ibid.*]

How remarkable! A twelfth-century appeal to the principle of human dignity - a principle which, in Jewish tradition, is a *point of law* and is not left to the realm of ethics or judicial sensitivities. Human dignity, a concept brought to the world through Torah, underlies a good deal of our legislation. In this regard, we have always insisted that excessive punishment degrades the offender—

When there is a dispute between men and they go to law, and a decision is rendered declaring the one in the right and the other in the wrong...the guilty one may be given up to forty lashes, but not more, *lest being flogged further, to excess, your brother be degraded before your eyes.*[25] [*Deuteronomy* 25:13]

And what shall we say about the appearance of impropriety? The media are replete with accounts of questionable behavior on the part of our officials. The matter of the appearance of impropriety occupies a great deal of the interest of our jurisprudential system and, quite significantly, what we might consider slight and even negligible behaviors are raised to the level of greatest seriousness — so much so that judges are asked to recuse themselves in the instance of such behaviors —

> . . . Not only is a bribe of money forbidden but also a bribe of words. It happened once that a judge was crossing a river on a small fishing boat, when a man stretched out his hand and helped him get ashore. The man had a lawsuit but the judge said to him, "I am disqualified from acting as judge in your suit."

> It also happened that a man once removed a bird's feather from a judge's mantle; another man once covered spittle in front of a judge. In each of these instances, the judge said: "I am barred from trying your case." . . . There is still another incident of a tenant farmer who, on Fridays, used to bring to the owner figs from the garden he was cultivating. On one occasion, however, he brought the figs on Thursday, because he had a lawsuit. The judge however said: "I am barred from acting as judge in your case," for though the figs were his, since the tenant brought them ahead of time, he was ineligible to try the case. [23:3]

---

[25] Fearing this requirement might be violated, even inadvertently, Jewish law has established a maximum of *thirty-nine* lashes!

The Jewish people have developed a long and venerable legal tradition which has become, through the centuries, a remarkably vibrant and creative system.   In the three thousand years of documentation available to us, there are to be found numerous concepts, principles and values which have contemporary relevance and applicability.   Jewish jurisprudential thinking offers some meaningful and potentially far-reaching direction and insights at a time when law and its institutions are suffering a deterioration of public confidence. And the voices of our prophets still call out to anyone who would listen —

> He has told you, O human, what is good and what
> the Lord requires of you: only to do justice, to love
> goodness and to walk humbly with your God.
> [*Micah* 6:8]

THOU SHALT TEACH THEM DILIGENTLY TO THY...SELF!

We delude ourselves dangerously every time we talk about doing something Jewish *for our children.* Our traditional literature is replete with allusions to children and the younger generation. With the completion of Pesah every year, I suppose you, like all the rest of us, take great pride in how our youngest were able to recite the Four Questions and how we entertained some lively discussion around the theme of the Four Sons (always presumed to be *children,* by the way). Pesah, surely in most Jewish homes, has contributed mightily to reinforcing the notion that, in the final analysis, Judaism is for the sake of the children. We'll do just about anything for our kids! We spend significant money for their education, we drive innumerable car pools for their transportation and we continually appeal to the sentiments of potential Federation contributors by harping on the theme of the Jewish education of our children. We have found in America a kiddie-centered culture and a social attitude which appeal strongly to the child-focused attitudes we Jews have held from the earliest times in our history.

A second factor contributing heavily to our strong commitment to our children's Jewish education is the largely negative conditioning we have experienced ourselves. I have recalled before the interminable boredom and gross irrelevance of the Hebrew School and Sunday School classrooms you and I have sat in. I will never forget the admiration I had for all those lucky Gentiles who did normal things after public school like ride bicycles and play ball and roller skate while I longingly watched them from the narrow windows of a stifling 4PM classroom, practicing the correct Hebrew phrases for asking a Tel Aviv bus driver to give me an ice cream cone. How many of us, early on, resolved not to submit ourselves ever again to (ecchhh) Jewish education? But (and is there any sadism in all this?), we also resolved when *we* became parents our children would!

They would be our proxies and *they* (because soooo much improvement has come about in Jewish education) would pick up where we had left off and *they* would secure the future of the Jewish people. Think about how many times this notion is consciously or subconsciously reinforced every time we read the *Shema*: "...and thou shalt teach them diligently to thy *children!!*"

These misbegotten notions have the very real potential for killing off the Jewish people; we live with a Jewish-American mythology which blinds us to the realities of our circumstances and forestalls the taking of redemptive measures. Consider if you will the fact that most of the people making decisions for the Jewish community are the war-wounded of Hebrew and Sunday school. Consider the fact that the greater part of policy formulation and decision-making for the American-Jewish community is in the hands of people who have had a *negative conditioning in their own Jewish upbringing!* Consider if you will the paltry pool of *JEWISH* understanding (values, concepts, ideas, beliefs, Torah, etc.) available to those who manage contemporary Jewish life.

We cannot continue to live our Jewish lives through our children and we cannot continue to presume that our Jewish future can, in any significant way, be secured by a new generation which will be "more loyal and more enlightened than we were." Count up the intermarriages and the apostasy and marginality of all those people (and relatives) you know — isn't it apparent that our most pious wishes have failed?

Basically, the answer is so simple. The FIRST responsibility for Jewish learning is with the *adult* community, with the very people who hold the reins of power and influence. It is to us that the younger generation looks and it is we who are, willy-nilly, the models for our children. They want to know what *we* think is important and they are judging us not at all by what we say but by what we do. They know words are cheap and they know that, for us, money is no object. They're not impressed — but they are deeply moved by what we do with our *most precious* commodity — TIME. How do we spend our time and how does what we spend our time with affect how we live and what we live for?

Jewish decision-making and Jewish policy formulation are directly enabled by Jewish learning and the elementary truth is that when adult Jews deeply and seriously study Jewish tradition, the *Judaization* of our institutions will be axiomatic. We will know what the priorities are in Jewish life because we will have been students of Jewish life. We will make *Jewish* decisions and we will fashion *Jewish* policy because we will know *Jewish* sources. We will cease identifying a thing as Jewish simply because its author is Jewish and we will know that, in all circumstances, something is Jewish because of its content, its very substance, and not because of the ethnic or biological derivation of its author.

What we are talking about here is a dominant theme in our tradition and I find it truly remarkable that our literature gives so much *priority* to adult learning. On the quantitative level, more is said about *our own* obligation to learn than anything having to do with our children! A look at some of our sources can provide a refreshing re-emphasis about what should really be important in our lives. Contemplate the fact that the very Jewish tradition which placed paramount importance upon the obligation to honor and respect parents would then emphasize that —

> The study of Torah is greater than the honor due
> one's father and mother. [*Megillah* 18b]

The priority of adult learning is heavily underscored in Maimonides' *Mishneh Torah* —

> If a man needs to learn Torah and he has a son who
> also needs instruction, his own requirements are to
> be satisfied first. . . . [*Hilkhot Talmud Torah,* 1:3]

And should any of us (not likely, is it?) choose to argue that, after all, there *are* extenuating circumstances, there *are* good and rational reasons why we're not studying at this time — Maimonides reminds us [the brackets are mine] that —

> Every Jew is under an obligation to study Torah,
> whether he is poor or rich [so much for tuition],
> healthy or ailing [that takes care of fatigue], whether
> young or old [that answers to "my memory isn't
> what it used to be"]. Even if a person is so poor
> that he has to beg [or solicit donations from others
> and "call pledge cards"] or even if a person has a
> wife and children to support [that takes care of
> "after all, it's my work that enables me to contribute
> to the campaign in the first place"] - one is
> obligated to . . . set aside a definite period . . . for
> the study of Torah. . . . [*Ibid.*, 1:8]

And for anyone so bold as to argue that his or her current
involvement in Jewish activities precludes spending any more time
on study —

> If the opportunity of performing a particular *mitzvah*
> would interrupt the study of Torah and the *mitzvah*
> can be performed by others, then one should not
> interrupt his study. . . . [*Ibid.*, 3:4]

How about the complaint that so many Jewish adult learning
opportunities are offered at night, after a long and tiring day and
after all one's strength has been spent in work and children and
telephone and chores and all the other things that make evening
hours "crash time"? —

> Whoever studies at night — the Divine Presence is
> with him. [Babylonian Talmud, *Tamid*, 32a]

How about those of us who say "I've had enough; really now, I've
gone through it already"? —

> You who have studied Torah in your youth, study
> Torah in your maturity! [*Avot d'Rabbi Natan*, 3]

Indeed, there is no way out, not in the view of our Sages
and not in the thoughtful review of what we have learned about the
source of our longevity, our vitality, our optimism and our vision
for what we and the world *can* be. And when we're done, when

it's all over and we've given up our earthly existence, when we're through with meetings and carpools and solicitations and memberships, what will it all have meant? —

> At the Judgment in the Hereafter, a person will first be called to account for his fulfillment of the *mitzvah* of the study of Torah and afterwards to account for his other activities. . . .   [*Hilkhot Talmud Torah,* 3:4]

R.J.REYNOLDS DOESN'T CHEW GUM

What does it mean to say you really believe in something? Not long ago, an executive with one of the big tobacco companies was being interviewed on television (CNN, I believe) and although I can no longer remember anything of the substance of the interview, I do indeed have a deep, lasting recollection of that executive's holding and smoking a cigarette throughout the interview. As a reformed cigarette smoker (ten years now!!), I suppose such portraits would be expected to impress me but, upon rethinking the matter, I came to the conclusion that what was really remarkable was the bold (and natural) display of the exec's commitment to his product.

Certainly, in recent years, the environment for smokers has become more hostile and, what with health reports, laboratory research and an aggressive Surgeon General, more and more smokers have come to be on the defensive. Not this guy! Puffs of smoke surrounded him as he spoke, and he simply spoke on. The smoke annoyed me (even though I couldn't smell it) and I remembered thinking, as I watched him, how obnoxious this habit had become to me (passion of the convert, yes?). But . . . I also admired this man -he believed enough in himself and in his product to use it publicly and to be identified with it. That set me thinking. Lee Iacocca drives a Chrysler. Frank Perdue eats chicken. The more I thought about it, the more I was impressed with the great number of people I know who truly believe in what they sell and whose selling is greatly enhanced by the mere (*mere?*) fact that they put their use where their loyalties are.

Then I thought about more people I know, people connected with products much more significant than cigarettes or automobiles or chickens. I began to think about all the board members and presidents and chairpersons of all those Jewish committees. I began to think about all those people who belong to (and work *hard* for) education and service and community organizations. I began to think about all the well-meaning members of the Jewish *leadership* community who may have been communicating a negative message for a long time without even realizing it. How many of these people, I ask myself, USE the very product they are selling — how many are involved, in an ongoing way, in studying Judaism in some formal class, somewhere? How many are taking advantage of *any* of the learning resources in their own communities to broaden their grasp of the very Judaism they say they love? How many realize that the unspoken message is often enormously more powerful than the spoken one and that the younger people of our communities are enormously impressed by what they see their elders do? That people in their thirties, forties and fifties take time out of their busy lives to apply themselves to a serious encounter with the sources of the Jewish tradition says more about values and priorities than dozens of posters and hundreds of blurbs in community newspapers.

I wonder how many corporate boards out there in America would favorably countenance the refusal of a director to wear, eat, or drive the very product the company touts and the very product for which the company was organized in the first place?

We who care are in a position to make a simple and yet far-reaching alteration in the way we do our community business. How about, if from now on, we establish a policy which obligates all officers and members of Jewish education services, committees, agencies and boards to study something Jewish on a regular basis — a policy which offers volunteer service positions *only* to those people who commit to using the product of the firm they work for? If the product isn't good enough to use yourself, then why should anyone else be expected to do so?

OPHTHALMOLOGY AND JURISPRUDENCE

Perhaps no other Torah verse has been more misunderstood and misrepresented than the phrase "eye for eye" in *Exodus* 21:24 (as well as *Leviticus* 24:20 and *Deuteronomy* 19:21). Several factors seem to have come together through history to explain the gross misunderstanding. Firstly, a strong antinomian sentiment in some of the literature of the Christian Bible contributed to the growth of a negative view of the sense and thrust of Torah. The essence of this matter is perhaps best illustrated by *John* 1:17 — ". . . the Law was given through Moses, but grace and truth came through Jesus Christ." In the succeeding centuries of the evolution of Christianity, Judaism was often characterized as tenaciously holding to the harsh law of a wrathful God while, in contrast, the God of the "New Covenant" embodied love and compassion.

Secondly, the diabolization of the Jewish people sustained the ongoing process of depicting Jews and Judaism as cruel, anti-Christian and unrelenting in their pursuit of a severe, perverse justice (remember Shylock's "pound of flesh"?).

Thirdly, plain old antisemitism (whether or not derived from Christian Scripture and the Church Fathers) found much justification for its malignity in the highlighting of verses such as *Exodus* 21:24.

Have you observed that, almost invariably, the phrase "an eye for an eye" is used by the media to describe some act which has occurred in a Jewish context? Most often, the phrase is employed to characterize military reprisals by the Israel Defence Forces or some other move by the Jewish State in which punishment is meted out against a non-Jewish real or alleged perpetrator. Incidentally, I believe I have identified the *only* media use of this phrase in a non-Jewish context and I record it here for posterity and for the purpose of illustrating the principle that "the exception proves the rule" — The New York Times of Wednesday,

February 20, 1991, in reporting the reaction of Nicaraguan crowds at the killing of former contra rebel leader Bermudez, observed that 1,000 former rebels broke through police cordons shouting "Eye for an eye! Tooth for a tooth!". Imagine my relief at seeing nothing Jewish in the article and imagine my further relief that dentists were not being excluded from formerly restricted ophthalmological territory.

The fact is that the Torah principle "eye for eye, tooth for tooth" represents yet another of its legal revolutions. Torah law, when seen against the background of prevailing ancient pagan law, reveals cosmically-significant departures from non-Israelite practice, departures which establish Torah law as the single greatest document of human liberation and affirmation of life. (Consider that Torah eliminated forever the idea that any property violation could ever be a capital offense!). Jewish tradition has *never* understood the dictum "eye for eye" as referring to anything other than monetary compensation — our concern for precision in law made it apparent that one could not literally take another's eye; think of all the uncontrolled variables (acuity, blood loss, pain, intrinsic value, etc.) With the exception of some brief moot argumentation to the contrary, Jewish jurisprudence has always read the Torah as meaning "the *value* of an eye for an eye." Moreover, the legal revolution implicit in the Torah verse is that THE PENALTY SHALL NEVER EXCEED THE CRIME — in an ancient world of varying and class-determined penalty (Code of Hammurabi, the Hittite Laws, etc.), the Torah says that *offense and penalty* must be equal and that the exacting of, for instance, a *life* for an *eye* is contrary to God's will.

The irony in this case is almost overwhelming. Our detractors seek to use the phrase "eye for eye" to denigrate and invalidate us while, at the heart of the matter, Judaism is the author of that very sublime legal concept which much of the rest of the world has yet to reach, despite two thousand years of the doctrine of love.

HISTORY AND HUMANITY

At the Passover season when we recall the oppression of the Egyptians, the attempts of Persian antisemites to annihilate the Jewish people and the Roman repression of Judaism (Lag Ba'omer), we must provide ourselves with some perceptual correctives. It is all too easy (and tempting) to repudiate the Gentile world and maintain our indictment of its depravity. Throughout our history, we have introduced attitudinal correctives into our literature and ritual. The spilling of ten drops of wine at the Passover seder reminds us that much *Egyptian* blood was spilled before the Exodus and that our liberation came at great *human* cost. The book of *Esther* clearly and emphatically depicts heroic and benevolent pagans and portrays a moving reconciliation. It is truly remarkable and much to the credit of the Godliness of our people, that Judaism, despite all the trials and misfortunes of our long history, never developed (as did Christianity or Islam, for instance) a triumphalism asserting that in order to be considered worthy or justified, or to be saved, or to be validated, one had to be a Jew! Over and over again, the theme of the commonality of humankind, created in the divine image by a compassionate and merciful God, runs throughout Jewish tradition. Far from repudiating a lawless Gentile world, we remind ourselves that God has many sons and daughters:

> The Holy One, blessed be He, provides for all people and all nations according to their needs; not only for the righteous but also for the corrupt and even for those who do not yet know God. [*Mekhilta, Amelek, Yitro*[26]]

---

[26] The oldest collection of rabbinic legal narrative and exposition (called *midrash halakhah* in Hebrew) outside the Mishnah, this work is a commentary on the book of *Exodus* and was composed during the first several centuries of the Common Era.

MAKING LOVE AT SINAI

I find the approach of the festival of Shavuot always to be the perfect occasion for reexamining some of the sublime and unique aspects of Jewish tradition, which, perhaps more than ever, need a re-hearing among fellow Jews and the world at large.

The intellectual DNA of Western Civilization has been heavily influenced by Christian doctrine and no significant approach to understanding Judaism fully can be made without first recognizing this fact. When we speak of the "DNA" of Western Civilization we mean to point to those attitudes, influences, perceptions and mindsets which constitute the character and nature of the contemporary world in which we live.

Indeed, one need not be a Christian at all to have inherited outlooks and concepts which owe their origin to classical Christianity. One of these significant concepts is the notion that law and prescription in matters of human behavior are inferior to the more sublime, the more pure belief/faith in "getting right with God." This is called "justification" in Christian Scripture and derives from the Hebrew word which gives us *tzedakah,* [equity, righteousness] and *tzaddik* [righteous person]. Christian Scripture is replete with allusions to the superiority of faith/belief/love/grace (=affect) over law and among the most notable citations are:

> Know that a man is not justified by observing the Torah, but by faith in Jesus Christ. So we, too, have put our faith in Christ Jesus that we may be justified by faith in Christ and not by observing the law, because by observing the Torah no one will be justified. (*Galatians* 2:16)

It was not through Torah that Abraham and his offspring received the promise that he would be heir of the world, but through the righteousness that comes by faith. For if those who live by the Torah are heirs, faith has no value and the promise is worthless, because law brings wrath. And where there is no Torah, there is no transgression. Therefore, the promise comes by faith... (*Romans* 4:13-16)

Judaism, even in its most ancient manifestations, has never insisted that faith in God, or love of God are the necessary and indispensable elements in "getting right with God." On the contrary, a leading characteristic of our tradition is its focus on proper *behavior* as the criterion for identifying merit. Torah is conceived of as the record of God's will in terms of Jewish conduct and the means through which the relational contract between God and Israel, the Covenant (*Brit*) is realized. Most simply put, God's will is that we *do* God's will and the *doing* of God's will, through Torah, is how we "get right with God." The Jewish concept of Covenant is that our love for and our loyalty to God are manifest in what we *do*, not in how we *feel*. To place authentic religious experience and access to God on the level of affect, in the end, makes access to God, for most people, most of the time, fraught with failure. It is not within the realm of the *real* human experience to be able, at will, to turn on emotions of love or compassion or faith or belief. Affect does not arise on demand and a system which demands affect GUARANTEES THE FAILURE AND UNFULFILLMENT OF THE PRACTITIONER!

So pervasive is the concept of "love" in religious behavior in the moral traditions of Western Civilization, that it has intruded into our own ritual and liturgy. How many millions of our people have come, over time, after reading the translations of our Bible and prayerbook, to severely misconstrue Jewish ideas: "Thou shalt love the Lord thy God with all thy heart, with all thy soul and with all thy might." How often have we seen these words and how often, consciously (or even worse, subconsciously) have we been reconfirmed in the notion that *loving* God is a Jewish requirement? Many of our people have been led to develop a sense of the inferiority of their own spirituality through repeated confrontation with "Thou shalt love . . ." Assumed religious demands to FEEL have conveyed enormous senses either of performance anxiety or the conviction that the one praying is Jewishly defective! In classical Judaism, the word so often wrongly translated as "love" (*ahav*) really means "loyalty" and the word "heart" (*lev*) points to the locus of "thought" and NOT the Greco-Roman-Christian "love".[27]   The proper, authentic reading of the famous Torah/Prayerbook verse (*Deuteronomy* 6:5) in question is much more something like: "You shall demonstrate your *loyalty* to the Lord your God with all that you have" — your mind, your body and your possessions.

The world-renowned thinker and teacher Yeshayahu Leibowitz has made the profound observation that:

> The most characteristic quality of the life of the *mitzvot* is its non-pathetic nature. The life of the *mitzvot* does not rely upon the awakening of religious feelings and does not grant importance to a special spiritual impulse prompting unusual experience and actions. It constantly strives to establish the religious act — even in its more sublime manifestations — as a fixed pattern of fulfilled obligation. "Greater is he who is commanded and does than he who is not commanded and does" (*Babylonian Talmud, Kiddushin* 31a). And precisely this very nonpathetic tendency manifests a tremendous pathos. How vain and empty is the vaunted antithesis between the intense religious experience and the formalism of the *mitzvot*. . . . [28]

The expression "Love thy neighbor as thyself" is probably one of the most well-known of all biblical phrases. There can be no doubt that this has come about through Christian Scripture's

---

[27] See *English Is A Christian Language*, pp.18-22.

[28] *Contemporary Jewish Religious Thought,* Arthur A. Cohen and Paul Mendes-Flohr (eds.), The Free Press, 1987, p.69.

reporting that when Jesus was asked what the most important commandment was, he responded "Hear O Israel, the Lord our God, the Lord is One, thou shalt love . . ." AND "Love thy neighbor as thyself" (*Mark* 12:28ff.). Although Jesus certainly knew better, most of his followers in succeeding centuries have been convinced that he was the author of the statement, not knowing that it was taken from the Torah (*Leviticus* 19:18). More importantly, that Torah phrase, far from demanding affect, has always been understood by us as a *behavioral* obligation:

> All those matters of Torah and mitzvot you would wish others *do* for you, you should *do* for your kinsmen.[29]

Another quite significant aspect of the misunderstandings we are addressing is the implications of concepts of "love" and "law" for the amelioration of the human condition. It is the contention of our tradition that human welfare, societal soundness and *tiqqun olam* ("repairing a fractured world") are best, and most dependably brought about *not* by professions of compassion, mercy or love but rather from the shared sense of *obligation* — you might say SENTENCE AND NOT SENTIMENT. That feeling and inspiration might *eventually* happen in the performance of the religious act is never doubted, but in the interim, it is only the sense of *obligation* which will insure that God's will gets done. And, should one not be certain either of God, or His will, the necessary deeds will still be done — "Says God: Let them forsake Me if they will, but let them keep My Torah."[30]

The Apostle Paul set the tone for what would become a predominating theme in Christianity (and hence, in Western culture) and would manifest its influences well into our own day:

> . . . the sinful desires stirred up by the Torah were at work in our bodies, and all we did ended in death. Now however we are free from the Law,

---

[29] Maimonides, *Mishneh Torah, Laws of Mourning,* 14:1.

[30] *Midrash Rabbah, Lamentations, Introduction,* 3.

because we died to that which once held us prisoner.
No longer do we serve in the old way of a written
law, but in the new way of the spirit. (*Romans* 7:5-
6)

Here, in essence, is the mesage: the spirit liberates, but law
imprisons; love is life but prescription means death. Here, in
essence, is a primary contrast between the Jewish view of reality
and the Christian message and it is a contrast which any serious
person has to confront. It is a contrast which goes to the very heart
of how one views himself and his world, how society is organized
and how social policy is formulated. It is a contrast which speaks
volumes about the integrity and substance of any attempt to find
meaning in life and purpose in the world. Shall our sense of
spiritual fulfilment be shaped by behavioral obligation or shall it be
shaped by individual escape from LIMITS to LIBERATION? Our
answer is that Torah liberates, that human beings *need* limits and
definition and parameters and borders to establish a sense of self,
of being, of shape, of ability and that this sense is exactly what
makes one truly free. Freedom is access to the fulfillment of will.
It is in the *doing* that we gain merit; it is in the doing of the Will
of The Other that we find The Self, and it is in the desire to *do*
that Will that we find love.
　　The greatness of the moment at Sinai is that God made His
love for us manifest through Torah, that we might return that love
by doing His will.

TORAH AND THE ART OF MINDING
OUR OWN BUSINESS

The old antisemitic canard asks "What is the shortest book ever written?" to which the answer given is "Jewish Business Ethics." To be sure, antisemitism has never needed truth or facts to make its ugly points, but, nonetheless, the venom spewed on our mercantile practices has a particular sting because so many of our people, for so long, have been engaged in the world of business. Some while ago, during a lecture I was giving in a large and prestigious Episcopal church, one of the assembled asked, quite deferentially and with assurances that he did not dislike Jews, why so many Jews seem to be involved in economic crimes. I responded that I would be able to answer his question when people start identifying Charles Keating, jailed for the enormous Lincoln Savings bank fraud, as the Episcopalian that he is! There was raucous applause for my response and I knew that the point was made.

As a teacher of the Jewish Tradition, my concern is not so much for the perverse perceptions of the Gentile world as it is for *our own* understanding of and identification with our long, venerable and lofty behavioral tradition. The fact is that, for many, many centuries, Judaism has attended to even the most minute aspects of behavior in commerce, trade and economics and that, for many millions of our people through the ages, Judaism's teachings in these areas constitute not only wise advice, but behavioral obligation.

It is unrealistic to expect that, through some magical or momentous instance, there will occur a mass return to Jewish law and standards on the part of the multitude of our people. But it indeed is reasonable to expect that, for those who are interested in Jewish roots and the teachings of our Tradition, many will discover some relevant application of Judaic principals in our mundane lives. I have always believed and taught that while growing familiarity with our tradition will not likely revolutionize most Jewish lives, the chance that our behaviors and perspectives will be positively modified in some way is quite great, as has been demonstrated time and again in my work throughout the United States and Canada. At the very least, for those who believe that many aspects of our Tradition are no longer applicable to contemporary life, the Tradition can and does offer a significant sense of how what we do can be done better, of how much farther we and the world around us have to go in our search for social advancement and the amelioration of the human condition (*tiqqun olam).* For intelligent, aware people, for Jews who think they care about being Jewish, the most basic questions must be: how does Judaism impact upon my life, what is there in the Tradition that speaks to where I am? What is there in the spirit, in the theory, in the attitude of our heritage that contains some potential address to my own circumstances and needs? For people who share these questions, a look at just a few examples can be quite rewarding. The Torah says (more than three thousand years ago) that:

> When you sell property to your neighbor, or buy anything from your neighbor, you shall not wrong one another. (*Leviticus* 25:14)

And in the manner characteristic of our microscopic attention to Torah meaning and implication, we have understood (more than two thousand years ago) that the verse above means:

> Fraud is constituted by an overcharge of four pieces of silver in the twenty-four pieces of a sela, that is, one sixth of the purchase price. Until what time is [one suffering defraudment] permitted to retract? Until he can show [the purchase for an opinion as to its value] to a merchant or to his relative. . . . (*Mishnah,*[31] *Bava Metzia* 4:3)

---

[31] The first codification of Jewish law, composed in Israel and completed at about 225 CE. It is a legal expansion and illumination of the Torah as well as the normativization of post-biblical law and practice. It is the basis for what becomes the

Judaism teaches that behavior is prior both to belief and emotion. It insists that behavior be quantified in order to give the greatest assurance that it will be done. Judaism maintains that law and regulation should tend, in mercantile matters, to favor the *customer*. Indeed, it seems that Judaism has been the earliest fashioner of the concept of favoring the buyer and, in effect, has created the principle of *caveat venditor* , "let the *seller* beware" in a world largely operating on the principle *caveat emptor*. So much does Judaism defend the buyer that the Torah edict concerning honest weights and measures is expanded to most remarkable limits — the Torah says:

> Do not have two differing weights in your bag — one heavy, one light. {14} Do not have two differing measures in your house — one large, one small. {15} You must have accurate and honest weights and measures, so that you may live long in the land the Lord your God is giving you. {16} For the Lord your God detests anyone who does these things, anyone who deals dishonestly. (*Deuteronomy* 25:13-16)

and the Mishnah remarks:

> [. . . After emptying the measure] the seller must let three more drops drip to the advantage of the buyer . . . (*Bava Batra* 5:8)

Moreover, with its characteristic attention to detail, the Mishnah adds:

> The shopkeeper must clean out his measures twice in the week and polish his weights once a week and clean out his scales after every weighing. (*ibid.,* 5:10)

Two thousand years ago, our great Sages are arguing that the merchant —

Talmud (completed ca. 600 CE).

> . . . must let the scales sink down a handbreadth [to
> the buyer's advantage].   If he gave him exact
> measure he must give him his overweight - a tenth
> for liquid measures and a twentieth for dry
> measures. (*Bava Batra* 5:11)

Imagine! An economic tradition that not only promotes the
primacy of the customer's interest but even goes so far as to
quantify the amount by which the merchant is *obligated* to favor
the customer — and all this in reflection of the Torah's demand
upon us that we maintain honest weights and measures!!

More than a thousand years after the Mishnah (three
thousand years since the Torah appeared), the great Sage Moses
ben Maimon, in his monumental work *Mishneh Torah* in which he
organizes and explicates all accumulated Jewish law up to his own
time, observes that

> There is a positive commandment to adjust balances,
> weights and measures accurately and to calibrate
> them very carefully at the time of their manufacture,
> for Scripture says, "Just balances, just weights...shall
> you have" (*Leviticus* 19:36).   Similarly, in measur-
> ing land great care must be taken to calculate the
> area of land according to the principles laid down in
> the works on geometry, for even a finger's breadth
> of land should be regarded as if it were filled with
> saffron.   A land surveyor should not measure one
> person's share in the summer and another person's
> share in the winter because the rope shrinks in the
> summer. . . . (*Torts: Theft,* 8:1-3)

How remarkable — a tenet of religious behavior which mandates
that adjustments be made in instruments of measure to compensate
for climatological effects on expansion and contraction!

Leviticus' admonition above, ". . . you shall not wrong one
another," in the fullness of our understanding and in our desire to
do Torah's will, also becomes, quite understandably, an admonition
to refrain from wrongs caused by things spoken, witness:

Just as there is fraud by overreaching in buying and selling, so there is wrong done by words. Thus one may not say to another, "What is the price of this thing?" if he does not wish to purchase it. . . ." (*Bava Metzia* 4:10)

Oral deception is more heinous than monetary fraud because restoration is possible in the latter while no restoration is possible in the former, and the latter concerns one's money while the former affects his person. . . . (Maimonides, *Acquisitions: Sales* 14:18)

It is forbidden to deceive people in buying and selling or to deceive them by creating a false impression. A heathen and an Israelite are to be treated alike in this respect. If one knows that an article he is selling has a defect he must inform the buyer about it. It is forbidden to deceive people even by words. (Maimonides, *ibid.*, 18:1)

One of the revolutionary aspects of Torah is its establishing the values of human dignity and protection of the powerless as points *in law!* Some of the most ancient elements of the behavioral code of the Jewish people portray truly extraordinary addresses to humanitarian treatment, a treatment which is viewed as *prior* to all valid interest in property and capital.[32]

When you make a loan of any kind to your neighbor, do not go into his house to get what he is offering as a pledge. Stay outside and let the man to whom you are making the loan bring the pledge out to you. If the man is poor, do not go to sleep with his pledge in your possession. Return his cloak to him by sunset so that he may sleep in it. Then he will thank you, and it will be regarded as a

---

[32] See *Why Be Jewish*, pp.50-51.

righteous act in the sight of the Lord your God. Do not take advantage of a hired man who is poor and needy, whether he is a brother Israelite or an alien living in one of your towns. Pay him his wages each day before sunset, because he is poor and is counting on it. Otherwise he may cry to the Lord against you, and you will be guilty of sin. (*Deuteronomy* 24:10-15)

And should there be any temptation to regard the sources discussed in this essay as "the old days" or "the things we used to do but do no more," some reference to the work of Professor Aaron Levine can be both instructive and reassuring. Dr. Levine, a rabbi and Chairman of the Department of Economics at Yeshiva University has an intense interest, as do many of us, in the application of Judaic principles to contemporary life, especially in the realm of business and economics. Like many of us, Dr. Levine sees hundreds, even thousands of instances in complex modern life for the application of Torah, for the opportunity to live Jewish lives in the fullest sense of the term. Look what has become of a small part of a single small verse of the smallest book of the Torah —

You shall not place a stumbling block before the blind (*Leviticus* 19:14)

Even though the seller has no investigative responsibility in respect to the financial status of his customer, offering a reluctant customer an installment plan as a means of inducing him to purchase an item he feels he cannot afford clearly violates Jewish business ethics. To illustrate, suppose crystal dealer A shows B an exquisite crystal chandelier. B reacts with excitement and admiration, but turns ashen when informed of its price. Eager to make a sale, A offers B the opportunity to pay out the purchase over a year in monthly installments. B remains reluctant, admitting that while the installment plan would make the purchase feasible for him, his budget, in consequence, would suffer considerable strain. Reminding B once again of the aesthetic qualities of the chandelier, A repeats his offer, expressing confidence that B will somehow make ends meet, the chandelier purchase notwithstanding. B is now persuaded and concludes the purchase. Since the purchase allows B to live beyond his means, A's *persuasion* clearly amounts to ill-suited advice and violates the . . . interdict ["You shall not place a stumbling block before the blind"].[33]

If you like irony, you will savor the fact that, taken as a whole, Jewish tradition devotes more attention to norms of commercial and economic behavior than almost any other topic — in effect, it is one of the longest ongoing books ever written!

---

[33] *Economics and Jewish Law: Halakhic Perspectives,* KTAV/Yeshiva University, 1987, p.62

CELEBRATION

"Celebrate your festivals, O Judah"
[Nahum 1:15]

SING A SONG OF SONGS

The arrival of spring has been, for eons, the season for the celebration of love. As the natural world reawakens from its dormancy, as the reemergence of green and the reaffirmation of life and continuity become apparent, a renewed and revitalized anticipation of "all the good things in life" fills people's minds and spirits. We know that it's a wonderful time and, in this most remarkable sharing of our humanity with people and cultures all over the world, from times past and in our own day, we reawaken to a sense of promise. It is in this vein that Jewish tradition has shared, from earliest times, a common bond with humankind.

Then there is Pesah and like so many moments in Jewish life, we simultaneously celebrate both our shared humanness and our particular Jewishness. Indeed, this pattern of the celebration of the UNIVERSAL and the PARTICULAR is strongly characteristic of our peoplehood. In fact, I would argue that the celebration of the one to the exclusion of the other leaves us unfulfilled and incomplete. Failing to honor our *uniqueness* in a world of commonality keeps us from appreciating our *selves* and, similarly, focusing *only* upon our selves deprives us of the pleasure and reassurance of our common bond with the human family and with life itself! Hillel said it: "If I am not for myself, who will be for me; but if I am only for myself, then what am I?"

Behavioral sciences are teaching us now that much of what we have identified as the malaise of modern times, of the wide dissatisfaction with job, self and even life can be traced to our failure to reconnect with the basic fundaments of life. With enlightened *chutzpa,* I would call it the lack of Pesah! Those who know have been telling us to "stop and smell the roses" and I've been thinking that that's what Pesah is saying too. Fact is, we don't usually pause to ponder "what it's all about" and the merry-go-round of our daily lives seems to make it ever more unlikely that we will stop for a significant moment of pleasant reflection on what we really have.

A central feature of the celebration of Pesah is the recitation of the Song of Songs. Rabbi Akiva, almost two thousand years ago, declared the work to be the poetic metaphor for God's love of the Jewish people.[34] It is not surprising that for many centuries, the reaffirmation of that love has enabled us to hold on. But Rabbi Akiva knew, as did his colleagues, that the Song of Songs *also* celebrates the wonderful preciousness of our relationships with each other and with life itself.

THE SONG OF SONGS IS SINGING ABOUT SPRING AND THE SONG OF SONGS IS SINGING OF PESAH; THE SONG OF SONGS IS SINGING ABOUT US! —

> Now the winter is past,
> The rains are over and gone.
> The blossoms appear in the land,
> The time of pruning has come;
> The song of the turtledove
> Is heard in our land.
> The green figs form on the fig tree,
> The vines in blossom give off
> fragrance.   [2:11-13]

IT'S PESAH NOW AND THERE IS JOY AND BEAUTY AND AFFECTION ALL AROUND US! —

> I have come into my garden,
> My own, my bride;
> I have plucked my myrrh and spice,
> Eaten my honey and honeycomb,

---

[34] "The world has never had so much merit as the day on which Song of Songs was given to Israel; for all the [works of the] Hagiographa are holy but *Song of Songs* is the Holy of Holies." (Mishna, *Yadayim* 3:5). Rabbi Akiva who was tortured to death by the Romans in 135 CE as they crushed the Bar Kokhba rebellion, was one of the greatest luminaries in the Jewish constellation and is responsible for determining much of what Judaism would become.

Drunk my wine and my milk.
Eat lovers, and drink,
Drink deep of love! [5:1]

I'VE BEEN SO BUSY THIS YEAR THAT I ALMOST FORGOT
WHAT I WAS WORKING FOR! —
They made me guard the vineyards;
My own vineyard I did not guard. [1:6]

IT'S PESAH AND NOW I'VE REDISCOVERED THAT —
I have my very own vineyard. [8:12]

IT'S PESAH AND NOW I REMEMBER THAT —
I am my beloved's and my beloved is mine.
[6:3]

IT'S PESAH NOW AND I REMEMBER WHAT YOU ARE TO
ME —
Like a lily among the thorns,
So is my darling among the maidens.
Like an apple tree among the trees of the
forest,
So is my beloved among the lads. [2:2-3]

You have captured my heart
With one glance of your eyes. [4:9]

IT'S PESAH NOW AND SUDDENLY THOSE LITTLE
IMPERFECTIONS DON'T MEAN ANYTHING ANYMORE —
Every part of you is fair, my darling,
There is no blemish in you. [4:7]

IT'S PESAH NOW AND IT'S TIME TO COME HOME! —
Awake, O north wind; Come, O
south wind! Blow upon my garden,
That its perfume may spread. Let
my beloved come into the garden;
And enjoy its luscious fruits! [4:16]

HANUKKAH - CELEBRATION OF THE NON-NEGOTIABLE

In those days there came forth out of Israel Assimilationists who persuaded many saying: 'Let us go and make a covenant with the nations around us . . .' and the saying appeared good in their eyes. [*I Maccabees*]

Here it comes again! Whenever America gears up to be immersed in the celebratory orgy of the end of the year, once again, we Jews who care will be challenged in our perspectives. I think it's time to stop re-running those usual themes like "Hanukkah is not a Jewish Christmas," or "If it were not for Hanukkah there would be no Christmas" (even though there's a lot of truth here!). Something else has to be said in terms of Jews' finding renewed and refreshed meaning in living tradition.

All the recent studies reconfirm what many of us already know — American Jews continue to assimilate at a quickening pace; intermarriages remain high, serious Jewish learning remains low and active expression of Jewish identity and practice is attenuated.

We may indeed be our own worst enemies. In our deep desire to be accepted into American society, we have latched onto the theme of what we share in common with our Gentile neighbors. When, by the end of the 19th century, the phrase "Judeo-Christian tradition" had been devised by well-meaning Gentiles and we began to understand that the equivalence suggested by this term signalled a degree of acceptance of the Jew and regard for Judaism in

American society, the pull of the theme of "commonality" was accelerated. In succeeding decades, we generated volumes proclaiming shared ethical insights, commitment to justice, humanitarianism, *menschlichkeit* (untranslatable, sorry!) and commitment to family values. And now we live to see some of the fruits of this labor. The simple fact is that for many of our people, the message of commonality has helped to validate the cultural assimilation of the Jew into Gentile society — after all, if we share so much with them in so many important areas and if indeed we are so much like them, *then why not marry them?*

In fact, there is indeed much that commonly defines us but, after all, if we are interested in the perpetuation of *Judaism,* then our focus, at some point, must turn away from the common to the uncommon, for it is in the uncommon that much of our substance is to be found. We are NOT like everybody else; we do hold distinctly different values and perceptions of truth and our position papers for the perfection of the world are, in many ways, radically distinct from our non-Jewish fellow Americans.

Hanukkah is about being Jewish and Hanukkah is about what I'm prepared to fight for as a Jew. Hanukkah is about limits and definition. Hanukkah's about reassessing what is non-negotiable in my life...what I am ready to modify or reformulate in consequence of being a proud and loyal American; what, for me, is not up for grabs, not open to dilution or diminution or cancellation or violation. Hanukkah is about consulting the venerable traditions of our people rather than making autonomous decisions about what stays and what must go.

This seems to me to be what Hanukkah is urging — where will I draw the line between what is of essence in my Jewishness and what is not? Hanukkah calls the question about the configuration of my identity, the things that define my purpose and the things that define my concept of what my life is all about. Hanukkah is about those aspects of Judaism I can't do without and Hanukkah is about how much I can give away before I discover that I have nothing left. Hanukkah is about all the reasons not to marry out *despite* the fact that our non-Jewish compatriots are fine and worthy human beings. Hanukkah is about the vigorous rejection of policy for the Jewish community which is formulated and promulgated by the assimilationist self-interest of the decisors.

Hanukkah is about the celebration of unique Jewish values and perspectives — about how you *feel* as being far less significant for the world than how you *act* — about how obligation defined in law must be prior to a world governed by love — about how baboon livers and fetal tissue are God's gifts for sustaining human life — about how family and belonging must translate into social fabric and public policy — about how history and tradition and memory keep people from losing their minds and souls and how ritual and celebration tell your children more about what you want for them than any words could ever say.

MACRO YOMTOV...MICRO YOMTOV

One of the fascinating things about this advanced technological age is the proliferation of terms for all sorts of things we never thought about much. Computers, data banks, telecommunications, radio astronomy . . . to our great wonder and amazement, new fields of endeavor, new vocabulary, new jobs and...new perplexities come at us in what seems to be an ever-increasing barrage. And then, Yomtov also comes . . . a time for a bit of quiet reflection, a chance to get off of life's merry-go-round for a short while, a chance to enjoy family and friends . . . a few moments to rediscover life's small pleasures and meanings.

I was thinking. Rosh Hashanah is coming (no matter when you read this, Rosh Hashanah will *always* be coming) and soon it will be another year. Rosh Hashanah is coming and the most extraordinary global events are swirling around us. I can't help but feel sometimes that world events are just overwhelming and that, in the face of all that's happening, I am disappearing, insignificantly, into the margins of life. After all, with an entire world (and, depending on whom you read, an entire *cosmos)* in movement and transition and change, just how important anyhow can an individual person be?

Rosh Hashanah is coming and soon it will be a new year. Another year to be lost in the flurry of world events? Another year to be overwhelmed by events larger and greater and more significant than solitary little (!?) me? Another year to spend being pushed aside to the periphery by those greater things that *really* count? But wait a minute.

All year long I've been seeing the words MACRO and MICRO — macrobiotic, microcomputer, microeconomics and macro commands . . . all around me the words are flying fast and furious and I've almost missed the message. With all this talk about MACRO — the big picture, the larger view — I see there is corresponding mention of MICRO — the intense, focused, close-up view and then I begin to understand . . . I begin to see more clearly just what the Rosh Hashanah prayerbook (*mahzor* for you Hebraically-oriented folks) has been talking about...it's been saying it for a long time, but apparently it's taken until the 20th century to really see it. I learn that the celebration of the New Year cannot really be complete until *yomtov* has been grasped on *both* the macro and micro levels. It's in the mahzor that I begin to find the resetting of balance, balance in my perception and balance in my own notion of myself...indeed, the prayerbook is telling me something I just never listened to before . . . it's telling me that reality and wholeness and meaning and celebration are complete only when experienced for their MICRO and MACRO aspects, for the GENERAL and for the SPECIFIC, for the UNIVERSAL and for the PARTICULAR, for the COSMIC and for the PERSONAL, for the WORLD and for ME! Rosh Hashanah reminds me that I need the macro view:

> Today is the birthday of the world. Let us now praise the Lord of all. Let us acclaim the Author of creation . . . He spread out the heavens and founded the earth."

and Rosh Hashanah reminds me that for every ALL, there is an EACH:

> On this day we pass before You, one by one, like a flock of sheep. As a shepherd counts his sheep, making each of them pass under his staff, so You review each living being, measuring the years and decreeing the destiny of each creature.

"ONCE IN A PURIM"

Quite possibly, you've heard the expression, often in Yiddish (*einmohl a poorim*) — "once in a Purim" — an expression intended to convey something of the notion of the rarity of an event, the infrequent (and perhaps, unanticipated) occurrence of some moment or occasion. To be sure, in our tradition, Purim has always represented a time of mirth, of levity and, you might even say, of triumph. Who among us does not remember the masks, the costumes, the *hamantashen,* the carnivals and all the other trappings of one of the significant fun times of our Sunday School and Hebrew School youth? For how many years did we hear again and again the story of Mordecai, Esther, Ahashueros and Haman (boo!) — the colorful tale of danger and intrigue, of beauty contests and royal favor and Jew-hating evil and ultimate Jewish victory? And then, we began to grow up and, to tell the truth, to grow beyond the stories of our youth...perhaps to revisit them through our children and grandchildren but, really, to grow beyond the simplicity of these age-old stories.

Something interesting, and wonderful, happens though, when, in one's maturity, another look is taken and a bit of sincere contemplation is offered for those things we haven't had occasion to think about for a long time. Every so often an idea comes to mind and, as it were, helps make some sense out of what we thought senseless. We learn, for instance that there are *many* Purims in Jewish life (the Purim of Florence, Purim de la Señora, Purim of Cairo, Purim de los Christianos and Plum-jam Purim, to name a few) and that we Jews have had a historical penchant for commemorating and remembering significant events in our lives. All the Purims mentioned above (and there are many, many more) commemorate the salvation of a Jewish community, the cessation of disaster or the rescue of a family from life-threatening calamity — in all instances, the escape from harm and death to relief and salvation were marked with celebration and rejoicing and, in all instances, the celebrants wanted to make sure that future generations would not forget what had happened. This has led me to reconsider the meaning of the phrase "once in a Purim" — a phrase I had heard from my grandparents but never really understood. If anything, I was sure the phrase pointed to the *rarity* of an occurrence and it never dawned on me that beneath it all, something much more significant, much more substantial was to be found...the fact is that Purim *does come much more frequently than once a year* but the question is whether or not we know it! I think there are *many* Purims in our lives but all too often, we do not take the time to contemplate and *celebrate* them. On the personal level, on the communal level, on the Jewish people level. Like miracles, the question is not whether they happen anymore but rather whether we can *see* them.

"...NO LEAVENED BREAD SHALL BE EATEN, YOU GO FREE ON THIS DAY..."

Symbols constitute a very significant part of the human experience and surely we have all had occasion to be deeply moved and inspired by a symbol which we understand. Seeing our flag flying over an American embassy overseas, giving a warm hug of welcome to a good friend we haven't seen in so long; bringing home an aromatic bunch of flowers in honor of the Sabbath — our lives, Jewish and American are replete with emblems which have the power to say, more eloquently than most anything else, how we feel, what we are thinking and what's important in our lives. We have all seen how symbols and tokens can address and express very complex profundities where words just simply fail. One of my favorite scholars of religion, Mircea Eliade said it well: ". . . the world "speaks" in symbols, "reveals" itself through them . . . [a symbol] *reveals* something deeper and more fundamental. . . ."[35]

Symbols are precious and intimate because they make abstractions accessible; they provide the means for our having personal contact with *meaning.* One catch, of course, for a symbol to "work", is that the observer have some *understanding* of the associations and referents for the symbol — symbols just don't go anywhere without comprehension. Pesah ("Passover" to the uninitiated) is probably more replete with symbols than any other moment in the entire Jewish calendar (yes, even than Shabbat!) and it should not be surprising therefore that Pesah, in terms of celebration and significance has had such a tenacious hold upon the Jewish people.

One of the simpler ways (not always dependable, but here

---

[35] *Myths, Rites, Symbols - A Mircea Eliade Reader*, Wendell C. Beane and William G. Doty eds., Harper Colophon, 1975, p.347.

it works) of assessing the degree of importance the Torah assigns to a given subject is to observe the frequency with which that particular subject is addressed. One such recurrent theme is "leaven" (*chametz,* in Hebrew) and it is instructive to take a look at some significant passages:

> Seven days you shall eat unleavened bread, indeed, from the very first day you shall remove *leaven* from your houses; whoever eats *leavened* bread from the first day to the seventh day, that person shall be cut off from Israel. [*Exodus,* 12:15]

> You shall not offer the blood of My sacrifice with anything *leavened* and the sacrifice of the Feast of Pesah shall not be left over until morning. [*Exodus,* 34:25]

> Then Moses said to the people: Mark this very day on which you have left Egypt, the House of Bondage, for with power the Lord has brought you out from here. Do not eat *leavened* bread. [*Exodus* 13:3]

> Unleavened bread shall be eaten for the entire seven days, no *leavened* bread or *leavening* shall be seen in all your borders. [*Exodus* 13:7]

> For seven days, you shall not eat anything *leavened* [with the sacrifice] but rather you shall eat unleavened bread [with the sacrifice], simple bread, because in haste you went out of the land of Egypt — you should mark the time of your exodus from the land of Egypt all the days of your life. [*Deuteronomy* 16:3]

Why such a focus and why such a heavy emphasis on something which most of us (and even most of *them*) hardly think about much? The answer lies in the fact that here, the Torah is portraying leaven (*chametz)* as a powerful SYMBOL and once we understand the meaning of that symbol, all the pieces fall into place. Leavening, the process which causes dough to rise, is a process of fermentation. With the juices of fruits, fermentation ultimately improves the product (as any wine or cordial lover knows) and even if something goes wrong in the production process, you at least end up with vinegar! With grain fermentation, while initially the product is enhanced, ultimately it is destined to decay and become inedible. And it is the very idea of *decay* which prompts the Torah's rejection of leavening on Passover! Pesah is liberation and Pesah is rebirth. Pesah is the celebration of awakening springtime and of renewal. Pesah is the affirmation of life.

By remarkable coincidence, the Hebrew word for "leavened bread" looks as if it is related to a similar sounding word meaning "oppression" and the multiple associations of *chametz* run throughout Torah and the rest of our tradition:

My God, rescue me from the hand of the wicked,
from the grasp of the perverse *oppressor* (*chometz*).
[*Psalm* 71:4]

For *violence* (*chammetz*) has vanished, rapine is
finished and pillagers have perished from the land.
[*Isaiah* 16:4]

Learn to do good, seek justice; aid the *oppressed*
(*chamotz*)... [*Isaiah* 1:17]

Right the *oppressed* (*chamotz*) but not the *oppressor*
(*chometz*). [*Babylonian Talmud, Sanhedrin,* 35a]

There's even more! Jewish tradition goes beyond the idea of "leavened bread" as decay and oppression and sees the word for leavening (or yeast) itself (se'or) as meaning "corruption" and "impediment." Using the idiom "leavening in the dough" as meaning the tendency to do evil, the Palestinian Talmud reports a prayer which includes the thought:

. . . and may it be Your will, Lord my God and God
of my ancestors, that You smash the yoke of the

evil inclination from our hearts. You have created us to do Your will and we are obligated to do Your bidding. You are desirous and we are desirous, but what stands in the way? — the "leavening in the dough" (*se'or sheba'isah).* *[Berachot,* 33a][36]

There you have it. Take another look at all the associations with "leavening" and you see a spread of meaning ranging from decay and oppression, to violence and evil. And here you see the enormous suggestive powers of a few simple words! Of course we abstain from leavened bread on Pesah because the symbolic suggestions of leaven run counter to the spirit and essence of liberation. Of course we refrain from leaven because freedom will not wait, the moment is now. Of course we will eat only matzah because, like its simple components of flour and water, some of the profoundest truths are basic and unadorned.

Lastly, Jewish literature reveals another meaning for *chametz* which should not escape our attention. Since fermentation requires TIME to come about, the extended meanings of "to tarry, to be late, to miss an opportunity" (*hachamitz*) appeared. These extended meanings, together with a play on the words *matzah* and *mitzvah,* resulted in the composition of a beautiful religious thought:

'Be careful regarding the unleavened bread (*matzot*)'[37] — Rabbi Oshaiya said: "we can also read the word *matzot* as if it were *mitzvot* — just as we would not tarry (*hachamitz*) in the preparation of the *matzot* so we should not tarry (*hachamitz*) in the performance of the *mitzvot* — if the opportunity to do a *mitzvah* comes along, grab it!" [*Yalqut, Bo,* 201]

---

[36] "Leavening in the dough" means "the evil inclination in our minds" says Rashi in his commentary to *Babylonian Talmud, Berachot,* 17a.

[37] *Exodus* 12:17.

". . . LET NOT THE DESTROYER ENTER YOUR HOME . . ."

"People are returning to family rituals because the world is losing a sense of what's important . . . Family rituals help people affirm what their beliefs really are." So states Dr. Janine Roberts, family therapist at the University of Massachusetts and author of *Rituals For Our Time* (Harper Collins). Dr. Roberts' significant observation is but one more example of a growing body of thought and research brought to us by the human sciences. Sure, there was a time when sociological truths were self-evident in the way we lived and in the values we taught. Somehow, the rush and frenzy of modernity, our setting aside many aspects of vital, real Jewish living in exchange for the seductive allure of contemporary culture, have contributed to our becoming estranged from our own traditions and authentic Jewish way of life. Sometimes blessings come in strange packages! — now it is that very non-Jewish, secular world, the world of the human sciences, which has begun to contribute so heavily to our rediscovery of our own truths!

Dr. Barbara Fiese, a psychologist at Syracuse University has observed that ". . . a family's rituals give children a sense of security and how their family works together, which is crucial in their own sense of identity."[38] Many, many psychologists and family therapists now energetically speak of the enormous importance of *family meals* and see the occasion of simply (simply?!) eating together as one of the most important reinforcements of family cohesion and validation. John E. Burkhart said it well when he argued "Quite simply, symbolic activities are actions that speak for themselves. Like hugs and kisses, they do not need to be explained, certainly not by words, and yet they are

---

[38] *New York Times*, March 11, 1992.

carriers of meaning, often shaping our lives in ways of which we are not fully conscious. To be human is to act symbolically and to symbolize through actions . . . As Suzanne Langer observed, human life 'is an intricate fabric of reason and rite, of knowledge and religion, prose and poetry, fact and dream. . . .' The primary question about ritual is not 'What does it do?' but rather, 'What does it say?' Ritual is essentially dramatic. It has a symbolic character, and functions in ways that practical activities do not. In Edmund Leach's lucid phrase, 'we engage in rituals in order to transmit collective messages to ourselves.' Therefore, . . . if you would know a people, would know what motivates them, would know what they really care about, study their rituals. Rituals reveal the convictions a society has about life."[39]　And all this *does* have a lot to do with Passover!

It is instructive to revisit the Torah's discussion of Pesah (the term much to be preferred over the alien label "Passover"). In outlining that one-time event known in our tradition as "The Pesah of Egypt," the Book of *Exodus* (c.12) directs that all ritual take place in the home, that the celebration be a *family* event in the context of the *home* ("none of you shall go outside the door of his house until morning") where all the celebrants are safe from the depredations of the world outside (". . . the Lord . . . will not allow the Destroyer to strike your homes.") In contemporary terms, we might say, along with Robert Gordis, that "the preservation . . . of a community is in the largest measure dependent not upon the credal doctrine or the ethical teaching which it shares, but upon its system of ritual and ceremony."[40]　For all the Pesah celebrations since Egypt, our children are expected to query family ritual ("What do you mean by this rite?") so that they may be told, among other things, that "God saved our homes."

Possibly no other momentous occasion in Jewish life is as replete with ritual as the Pesah *seder* and the fact that this observance revolves around home, family, meal and celebration should underline our interest in the thinking of psychologists,

---

[39] *Worship,* Westminster Press, 1982, pp. 23-4.

[40] *A Faith For Moderns,* Bloch, 1960, p.283.

cultural anthropologists, sociologists and others. Not long ago, Theodor Reik, renowned student and colleague of Freud, in speaking of ritual and religious custom, observed that "The character of *action* which is such a marked feature of ritual may be more profitably investigated psycho-analytically than the ideas, commands, prohibitions, dogmas and complicated sentiments, which later have become the chief content of religion. . . . The remarkable vitality which has enabled the Jews to weather all storms and to maintain their existence as a distinct people constitutes a problem that cannot simply be explained on biological or historical grounds alone; mental factors must have cooperated in producing such a result."[41]

Important for us is the understanding that when we speak of ritual, and especially when we speak in the context of Pesah, we mean to emphasize the practice of ritual in the HOME. For all too many Jews, the synagogue is viewed as the proper locus for ritual celebration and it is one of the sad facts of modernity that we have allowed the synagogue to become the proxy for what properly should be happening in the home! In many areas, the synagogue has become the surrogate for the home, and this surrogacy has contributed mightily to the demise of those benefits and satisfactions which only the intimacy of home celebration can provide. Needless to say, this self-same surrogacy has been instrumental in reducing rabbinic functioning to that of *vicar* whereby religious and ritual obligation is fulfilled through him rather than by each individual. It seems to me that as we rely more upon the Rabbi for the execution of such obligation, we bring about a corresponding decrease in the frequency and intensity of personal practice and the *home* becomes less and less the focus of those religious behaviors which enrich and protect us.

Compounding the problem is the widespread alien notion of hypocrisy, that destructive and insidious concept which we have borrowed from the Gentile world urging that, in the realm of religious practice and behavior, "if you don't do it all, then just

---

[41] *Ritual: Psychoanalytic Studies*, Norton, 1931, p.16 ff.

doing some is hypocritical."[42]   This attitude prevails (spoken or not) over such things as lighting Shabbat candles in a non-Sabbath observing household, attending synagogue on an irregular basis, or performing ritual or ethical rites in a home where the celebrants are not God-believers.   More than any other factor, this wrongly-appropriated, foreign notion of "hypocrisy" has convinced many Jews that doing nothing particularly Jewish is decidedly better than doing only some ("Who wants to be a hypocrite?").   The real truth is that Judaism teaches resolutely and emphatically that each and every *mitzvah* has its own virtue and that this virtue is not dependent upon whatever else the performer is or is not doing. Our obligation is to do *more*, but our merit is not dependent upon doing it *all*. Our performance is dictated by the very fact of our being Jewish and belonging to the Jewish people.   Absolute consistency, total performance and belief in God are neither prerequisites nor qualifications for living Jewish lives, sharing Jewish values and inculcating a Jewish way of life in our children. If we can only get over the inhibitions and awkwardness foisted upon us by this monster *hypocrisy,* reasserting our senses of self-worth and integrity and desiring to do what is good and upbuilding and fulfilling for ourselves and our families, then we shall have taken the most significant of steps in repudiating and protecting against the "destruction which is outside our homes."

---

[42] See "*I Don't Want To Be A Hypocrite*," pp.21ff.

"DOIN' WHAT COMES (UN)NATURALLY"

An outstanding characteristic of Jewish tradition is its relentless grappling with the realms of the "natural" and the "unnatural." Certainly throughout much of our classical literature, our struggle with this duality can be clearly seen and it is this very struggle which provides us with some remarkable insight into unique Jewish perspectives on life and reality.

Even in such early documentary sources as the Creation Stories of Genesis this portrayal is observable. The first chapter of Genesis reports that "God blessed them (male and female humankind) and God said to them: Be fertile and increase, fill the earth and *master* it and *rule* the fish of the sea, the birds of the sky and all the living things that creep on earth" [v. 28] - making undeniably clear our ancient understanding that control and domination of the natural world are not only divine mandates, but that such control and domination are, in themselves, characteristics of divine behavior! The narrative of *Genesis* 2 (the "Adam and Eve" story) reports that "The Lord God took the Man (Adam) and placed him in the Garden of Eden, to *till* it and *tend* it — pointedly employing the verbs "to till" and "to tend" so as to reflect a further refinement of this dual conception of the human commission — to care ("tend") for the natural world and also to work ("till") it — to enjoy the bounty of nature and yet also to *exploit* its potentials. "Tending" is *stewardship* while "tilling" is *manipulation* — and *both* functions have divine mandate!

Judaism is the record of our long experience in managing this grand duality and it is in our recognition of the supremacy of God and the concomitant empowerment of man that we continue to define ourselves and our relationships. Consider if you will how many examples there are of our approach to the duality of stewardship and manipulation and how, most importantly, *manipulation* is laden with the most profound significance.

Consider, if you will, that male circumcision is, in its very essence, the violation of the *natural* state of the human body and yet how circumcision, an unnatural (we might say, *transnatural)* phenomenon becomes, for the Jew, an ultimate declaration of our allegiance to divine sovereignty —

> God further said to Abraham, "As for you, you and
> your offspring to come throughout the ages shall
> keep my covenant.   Such shall be the covenant
> between Me and you and your offspring to follow
> which you shall keep: every male among you shall
> be circumcised . . . and that shall be the sign of the
> covenant between Me and you." (*Genesis* 17:9-11)

It is in the *alteration* of the natural that the sense of human worth can be so clearly articulated. We are forbidden to desecrate the body[43] and, at the very same time, are bidden to sanctify it through modification.

We celebrate God's bounteous agricultural gifts at the harvest festival of Sukkot and yet, the sukkah itself, a primary symbol of the occasion, is valid for use *only* when the natural materials of which it is constructed are no longer attached to the trees and soil from which they come. What a magnificent paradox — we celebrate God's gifts of the natural world and, in that very celebration, use materials which have been irretrievably altered by the celebrants! The same, of course, is true of the palm branch (*lulav),* the citron (*etrog),* the myrtle (*hadass)* and the willow (*aravah)* — in *every* instance, if any of the symbolic accoutrements of the festival are left still attached to their natural sources, they *cannot* be used to celebrate the festival — for true celebration is in the *partnership* of God the Creator and Human the Fashioner.

The occasion of Rosh Hashanah and Yom Kippur provides a wonderful example of the deeply significant way in which we attempt to integrate the duality of the natural/transnatural into our lives. Rosh Hashanah, among other things, celebrates the birthday of the world and, as such, celebrates an occasion which itself is

---

[43] See, for example, *Leviticus* 19:27-28.

determined by the *natural* world — solar and lunar cycles come together to define the broad outlines of the period. Autumn rains and changes in agricultural cycles dictate the circumstance. On the other hand, Yom Kippur exists not because of any periodicity built into the universe but *only* because of our intention to establish a moment of spiritual significance! The seasons of the year would exist even in the total absence of human beings but The Day of Atonement exists only because *we* have made it so![44]

And thus we are able to come to some pivotal understanding of the concept and institution of Sabbath in Jewish life. From one aspect, the Sabbath is *transnatural* — there is nothing at all in the inherent functioning of the universe that dictates that the twenty-five hour period from Friday evening until Saturday evening be Shabbat — Sabbath exists only because *we*, through our celebration of it, give it existence and it is through our giving it its existence that we verify and manifest our indelible relationship with the Creator of the Universe. It is in the celebration of the *transnatural* that our allegiances become manifest; it is in the self-imposed obligation to norms of behavior and conduct that we attest to God. If Shabbat were part of the cosmos, then its celebration would be self-evident. That Shabbat exists *only* by virtue of our intention, speaks eloquently to our concept of a Divine/Human partnership. It is through our choice of the *transnatural* that we lend definition to our concept of human significance. We *choose* to desist from mundane activity on the Sabbath; we choose not, as much as possible, to disturb the natural routine of the world around us — we do not plant, we do not harvest, we do not shop and we do not cook; we do not toil and we do not labor; we do not destroy and we do not build; we do not fashion and we do not alter. On Shabbat we recover that sense of our mandate to *tend* — this day we do not *till* —

---

[44] It is most noteworthy that the transnatural occasions of our tradition are seen as so laden with significance that their violation (labor on the Sabbath, remaining uncircumcised, eating leaven on Passover, not fasting on Yom Kippur) calls for the death penalty or social excommunication.

The Israelites shall *tend* the Sabbath, thereby rendering the Sabbath, for all their generations, an eternal covenant. (*Exodus* 31:17)

For us, Shabbat is not what we *cannot* do but rather what we *choose* not to do. For us, Shabbat is the laying aside of mastery and domination, a time to rejoin the natural rhythms of our world, a time to rediscover the joy of being free, the joy of being a creature and in so doing, to rediscover our wondrous God-given ability to achieve holiness.

WHAT'S A JEWISH WEDDING?

The more I attend *Jewish* Jewish weddings, the more I am impressed with all that is lacking in the mundane, popular versions. Recently, at the marriage of the son of old, dear friends, for reasons I will perhaps never know, right in the midst of the merrymaking, I began to think of all the things so many of my people will never know.

The bride (yes, all brides are beautiful, but some....) was a convert to Judaism, drawn to God and Torah long before any nuptial involvements. I was transported, in my memory to another wedding several years ago where a student of mine married an Italian Catholic convert and where the klezmer band played tarantellas in which bearded Hassidim, *tzitzit* flying, outdanced the family of the bride.

Returning to the present occasion, I struck up a conversation with a Catholic priest, an uncle of the bride and began to explain some of the celebration he was seeing. As the groom slowly walks down the aisle on his way to the *huppah* (nuptial canopy) each row of attendees before him rises to their feet; they sit and then the bride paces her way to the *huppah* - once again each row of well-wishers stands as she approaches, then they sit for the continuation of the ceremony. "Why do the people stand for the bride and for the groom as they enter?" the priest asks me. "Because today," Father, "they are King and Queen and we rise in homage, acknowledgement and respect." He understood.

The ceremony draws to a close, a small glass, wrapped in a napkin, is placed at the feet of the groom who proceeds to crush it beneath the sole of his shoe. "What is the meaning of this?" asks Fr. John. Quoting *Psalm* 137, I respond "Let my tongue cleave to the roof of my mouth if I do not remember thee, O Jerusalem, if

I do not set thee above my chiefest joy." He understood.

Impromptu choirs of young people serenade the bride and groom with songs of Jerusalem and happiness and long life and God. Dignified and respected Rabbinic scholars and heads of Yeshivot dance before the new husband and wife with as much energy and abandon as any twenty-year-old. At these happiest moments, tears well up in the eyes of those who, like myself, see this wedding as a clear and substantial proof that Judaism and the Jewish people will prosper and prevail.

I mentioned that the dancing taking place in front of the seated bride was a practice of great antiquity (Catholics, I thought, more than many other Christians, would have a great appreciation for antiquity.) I pointed out to my interlocutor that the fervid dancing he was seeing was not only the expression of happy friends and family of the newlyweds, it was also done in fulfillment of the Talmud's insistence, two thousand years ago, that the attendees do their very best to make the bride happy:

> *Kaytzad M'raqdin Lifney Hakalah*
> How do we dance before the bride?
> [Singing] O Bride! Lovely and
> fair![45]

He understood.

Twenty different kinds of alcoholic beverages were served and consumed, yet no one was drunk. Hundreds of very happy celebrants, yet no tasteless sexual wisecracks. No limbo bar, no bunny hop, no deep-cleavaged frontless dresses, no garter toss, no erotic dancing. Much spirituality, much delicacy, much modesty, great happiness - happiness for the new bride and groom and therefore happiness for the Jewish people:

> *Od Yishama B'arey Yehudah* . . .
> Heard throughout the villages of Judea
> and in the streets of Jerusalem;

---

[45] *Babylonian Talmud, Ketuvot* 16b-17a.

The song of joy, the song of happiness;
The song of the groom and the song
of the bride.[46]

---

[46] *Jeremiah* 33:10.

ISRAEL

*"I will give your descendants all this land I
promised and they will possess it forever"*
[Exodus 32:13]

WHAT IS A JEWISH STATE?

Debate on the classic question continues. Real lovers of Zion remain committed to the proposition that Israel, as the Jewish State, can only be called such on the basis of its *functioning* as a Jewish entity in terms of values, principles and policy. A state cannot be called Jewish simply because its population is primarily that. In fact, I can think of no area of human endeavor where the product would correctly be labeled Jewish simply by virtue of the cultural or genetic identity of its producer. Political positions are not Jewish simply because their proponents are. Nor are medical ethics or music or books or paintings or ideas or good deeds. All the while we glibly bestow the designation "Jewish," we demean ourselves and vitiate the authenticity of what we stand for. I think that often, we rush to declare a thing Jewish either out of inordinate ethnic pride or out of a desire, in the world spotlight, to take credit for *anything* that looks halfway decent or is likely to impress Gentiles. Real Jewish means that the thing *flows* from the Jewish tradition and is a reliable and authentic manifestation of it.

I have lots of ideas about what might make Israel truly a Jewish state; I'm sure you do too. Whenever Marcia and I spend time in Israel, I am reminded that modern Israel is not yet even fifty years old, is still in its infancy and that I and all fellow Jews are, and must be, its nurturing parents. I am reminded that my anguish over policy for Judea, Samaria and Gaza is the anguish of parenting and that the Book of Joshua is followed, ultimately, by the Book of Isaiah (same child, different ages).

I am reminded that Jersusalem is much more our model than Tel Aviv, but that Tel Aviv is us, too. I am reminded that the newly-established cooperative settlement of Nofit (near Haifa) means that Zionism, idealism and Judaism are alive and well, that our friends Shifra and Ehud Kalfon (not among the knitted kippah wearers) build synagogues, raise Jewish children and pour out their love on gardens, trees, streams and birds . . . carefully managing the heights overlooking the Galil area where our Mishnaic Sages walked. I am reminded that I still cannot visit Hebron whenever I wish ("today is not such a good idea, maybe next week.") And I am reminded of the great pleasure of being able to dispense tzedakah at the Western Wall and the great sadness that I can still have that pleasure.

I am reminded that riding on the bus to Netanya, in the company of my people, is always a memorable experience. I am reminded that the aroma and taste of freshly baked rolls from a little shop on King George St. (*King George!?*) in the heart of Jerusalem are truly incomparable life pleasures. I am reminded that a somewhat chaotic political system is subject to change, that socialized industry is not necessarily the best economic plan and that Israel still has to allocate a greater percentage of its GNP for defense than *any other nation in the world.*

I am reminded that Israel sorely needs court systems that incorporate some of the loftier principles of *halakhah*, a social welfare policy which derives from our concept of *tzedakah* and engaging alternatives to a pervasive and soulless secularism. I am reminded that Israel, like all contemporary Jewry, as Martin Buber put it:

> . . . is in the throes of a serious religious crisis [and that] . . . the true solution can only issue from the life of a community which begins to carry out the will of God, often without being aware of doing so, without believing that God exists and that this is His will.[47]

I am reminded that, in the words of Martin Cohen:

> . . . the importance of the State of Israel for the internal mission of the Jews cannot be overemphasized . . . because from the very

---

[47] *Pointing The Way*, Harper, 1957, p.230.

beginning of the Jewish tradition the Holy Land formed the territorial component of the covenant between the people Israel and God.   The transcendent significance of the Land of Israel is indelibly stamped upon the psyche of all self-respecting Jews, even those who claim to be irreligious. To be sure, the State of Israel is not the ideal Messianic state promised in Scripture and Tradition. . . . Yet who will deny that it is the closest that we have come to the Messianic state for at least the past nineteen hundred years? And who knows but that it is the Messianic state in time that will yet develop into the Messianic state of eternity?[48]

The following observation was made in the New York Times several years back, covering then Foreign Minister David Levy's visit to China as a prelude to the mutual establishment of diplomatic relations:

Because of the Sabbath, Mr. Levy will not hold meetings on Saturday. Nor will he and his delegation be served any meat because of China's lack of kosher food.

I am reminded.......

---

[48] Leon Klenicki and Helga Croner (eds.), *Issues In The Jewish-Christian Dialogue,* Paulist Press, 1979, p.172.

THE JOY OF MOURNING

"Rejoice with her in joy, all you who mourn for her"

At first glance, this passage from *Isaiah* (66:10) seems to be every bit an oxymoron - what can rejoicing possibly have to do with mourning? Why would the two very distinctly opposite emotions share the same space in such an unusual sentence? What does this mixture of joy and gloom have to do, in particular, with Jerusalem? And, finally, what does all this have to do with the fast day of the Ninth of Av?

For two thousand years now, we have been putting Jerusalem in the forefront of our minds...the prayerbook, the *hagaddah*, in household decor and design, at weddings...in so many ways...it was the Jews, and it is the Jews alone, who have wept over the destruction of Jerusalem. It was the Jews, and the Jews alone, who vowed never to forget Jerusalem and it was the Jews alone who hoped and prayed for the day when all her children would return to her. For us, the loss of Jerusalem has meant the loss of Jewish sovereignty. For the Jews, the loss of Jerusalem has meant the uprooting of an indigenous people and consequent exile into alien lands. For us, the loss of Jerusalem has meant the severing of an intimate connection with God. For the Jews, the loss of Jerusalem has meant the prolonging of the pangs of the Messiah and for us, the loss of Jerusalem has meant the loss of the ultimate model for the idea of the beauty of holiness. For us, the loss of Jerusalem has meant the loss of home both for God and for His people.

Now we who have mourned for her have returned. Jewish sovereignty has been re-established in Jerusalem, signalling the "beginning of the efflorescence of our redemption." Tisha B'Av calls to mind the intimate connection between our past and our as-yet-unfulfilled future. And while we lament so do we reaffirm the promise of the exhilaration *which the Jewish people alone can know*:

> Only those who mourn for Jerusalem
> will ever merit seeing the joy of her
> (*Babylonian Talmud, Ta'anit,* 30b)

ISRAEL AS TREE

Every New Year is the occasion for revitalizing our vision and refreshing our hopes and anticipations for the future. This is certainly evident in our celebration of the calendrical New Year, Rosh Hashanah and, for those who know and understand, a central theme in the national New Year, Pesah. What about the New Year for TREES on the fifteenth of the month of Shevat? This occasion, Tu B'shvat, celebrates trees; and the timing for the occasion is determined by Israel herself, and only Israel — it is the time when the budding of her almond trees becomes apparent, heralding the certain coming of spring.

The tree, of course, is also a symbol, a rich emblem of Torah in terms of sustenance and nurture ("It is a *tree* of life for those who hold fast to it"[*Proverbs* 4:2]) and a metaphor for the actively loyal Jew (". . . like a *tree* planted by waters . . . its leaves are ever green, untroubled by drought" [*Jeremiah* 17:8].)

But the tree is even more — it is the token of the vision of a redeemed Jewish people AND a perfected Jewish state. In essence, it is a celebration of the Eretz Yisrael that is and the Eretz Yisrael yet to be — "Rabbi Hiyya, in the name of Rav Ashi, in the name of Rav said: 'In the future all the shade trees of Israel will bear fruit . . .'" [*Babylonian Talmud, Ketubot,* 112b].

That's the message for Tu B'shvat: *Every* tree contains within itself the potential to become a fruit tree . . . and some day it will!

TITLE, OCCUPANCY AND JEWISH HISTORY

The Jerusalem of This World is not like the Jerusalem of the World To Come — anyone who wants to come to the Jerusalem of This World comes — only those who are *invited* come to the Jerusalem That Will Be. [*Babylonian Talmud, Bava Batra,* 75b]

Events in the Middle East seem to be unfolding more quickly than our ability to absorb what is happening and to make sense out of what we know are truly momentous happenings. The Gaza Strip and Jericho have been ceded to Palestinian administration in what is only a first step toward an autonomous Palestinian state. For we Jews (and any other people of good will), the very thought of foregoing total and complete possession of Eretz Yisrael is unsettling, to say the least. What of our historic right to the whole of Israel? What about security matters? What of Judea and Samaria? What will come of the unity and integrity of Jerusalem, regained in 1967 at such great cost?

Now, as always, we need the assistance of larger perspectives and contexts to enable us to move on with our lives, continue to repair the world and pursue a Jewish vision of the future. I find that some very powerful resources in our tradition address directly our current concerns (so what's new?) and contribute enormously to our "making sense." How can we come to terms with the very likely prospect that our half-siblings, the sons and daughters of Ishmael will be moving in with us even though we don't really want them and even though the house is not quite large enough to contain two growing families? Well, the fact is, we just *have* to make room and the sooner we can identify some reasonable accommodation for the "new facts" the sooner we will be able to get on with our national destiny.

There can be no doubt, our title to Jerusalem and all of Eretz Yisrael is an absolute and irrevocable title:

> I give the land you dwell in to you and your offspring to come, all the land of Canaan, as an everlasting possession. [*Genesis* 17:8][49]

> Jerusalem encompasses all the Land of Israel. [*Zohar, Numbers,* 104][50]

It is we, the Jewish people, who have kept alive through the storms of history, our soulful hopes for returning to Israel and for resettling in Jerusalem. Despite exile and dispersion, our prayers, our prose and our poetry recall the Jerusalem of the Divine Promise. The utterance "Next year in Jerusalem" has made it consistently clear that no matter what happens to us, no matter where we are, no matter what others may choose to do or say, we have not at all relinquished our title (no chance here for others' claim of adverse possession, as the lawyers might say). Moreover, through the ages, there were always families of Jews living in the land in an unbroken chain of residency (however partial and restricted,) substantiating our claim to the *whole* (constructive possession, in real estate law).

So much for *title,* but occupancy is another matter! Now we are facing the very real prospect that peace and the end of the spilling of blood are within reach and that a new era of concord and adaptation can be achieved. The cost? Some real estate adjustments. Suppose the adjustments mean that some of our half-siblings move in with us in exchange for *sh'lom bayit,* domestic tranquility? And suppose that, in order to achieve domestic tranquility we start to talk about *occupancy* and stop getting hung

---

[49] See also *Genesis* 26:3; 35:12.

[50] Mystical commentary on the Torah and a major source for Kabbalah, Jewish mysticism; attributed to Rabbi Shimon bar Yohai (mid 2nd century, CE). The *Zohar* was first publicized through Moses de Leon (1240-1305).

up on matters of *title?*

And just suppose that, in a portion of the Old City, somewhere facing toward Salah ad-Din Street a Palestinian flag flies over a group of buildings housing Palestinian government offices and just suppose this flag and these offices are regarded by our half-siblings as the Capital of Palestine while at the same time we Jews turn our eyes and our hearts toward the Eternal Jerusalem, Capital of the Jewish State and fulcrum of Jewish peoplehood.[51] Just suppose we have to make a few occupancy adjustments (easements of necessity, you might say), squeeze a little closer together and share some of the utilities? A little crowded? Yes! A little uncomfortable? Yes! Not quite the way we'd like things to be? Yes! You can say the same for Gaza, the same for Jericho and the same for any other easements we might care to make . . .

> That there might be peace within your walls and
> security within your citadels, for the sake of my
> brothers (and half-brothers) and my friends I will
> say "Peace be within you." [*Psalms* 122:7-8]

But what has happened to the Eretz Yisrael of the Divine Promise and the Eretz Yisrael of the prophetic vision? How can we relent now and how can we continue to grant easements which only postpone our national fulfillment? We will remind ourselves, as we must, again and again that an incomplete Jerusalem and an incomplete Israel are the physical symbols of an incomplete Jewish history, of a Jewish destiny which still awaits the fulfillment of the Messianic promise ("God will descend to Jerusalem and renew the world from there").[52] More of the Divine Will waits to be accomplished — a truly *Jewish* state (in law, in business, in social policy, in education, in moral perfection) awaits our initiative. The Eretz Yisrael of today is *not* the Eretz Yisrael That Will Be and even the works of our hands are not the final measure of all things.

---

[51] "The rebuilt Jerusalem, a city *united*" [*Psalm* 122] - what does "united" mean? She *unites* all Jews one to the other! [*Jerusalem Talmud, Bava Qamma* 7]

[52] *Otiyyot d'Rabbi Akiba, Hey,* a collection of mystical contemplations following the twenty-two letters of the Hebrew alphabet; composed circa 700 CE.

The time will come when title and occupancy and possession and easement will be resolved by the Ultimate Owner —

> Then the mountain of the Lord's Temple will be established as chief among the mountains, it will be raised above the hills and all the nations will stream to it. Many peoples will come and say, "Come, let us go up to the Mountain of the Lord, to the House of the God of Jacob. He will teach us His ways so that we may walk in His paths. Torah will emanate from Zion and the word of the Lord from Jerusalem. He will judge between the nations and will settle disputes for many peoples. Nation will no longer lift up sword against nation nor will they train for war anymore. O House of Jacob, let us walk in God's light! [*Isaiah* 2:2-5]

PAST AND FUTURE

"Remember the days of old; contemplate the years past"
[Deuteronomy 32:7]

WE HAVE MET THE ENEMY AND THEY ARE . . . US!

It's not so long ago, is it, when we were seated in Hebrew School and Sunday School learning, with some fascination and a great deal of anticipation (presents!) about the miraculous Hanukkah story? After the villainous Syrian Greeks were defeated, the Temple in Jerusalem was restored and a one-day supply of kosher oil for lamp lighting lasted eight full days, establishing thereby not only the miraculousness of the Hanukkah story but, importantly, securing what would later become an eight-day period of festivity and gift giving. In a word, we were taught in our youth that the two central points of Hanukkah were victory over foreign oppression and miraculousness in Temple re-dedication. Now we are a bit older; some of us are even a bit wiser but those deeply ingrained childhood recollections about Hanukkah linger on with the net effect that:

- we regard Hanukkah as a children's holiday
- we regard some significant moments in Jewish history as fantasy
- we fail to see a lesson of Jewish history which could save our collective lives!

The Hanukkah story as we have come to know it has been handed down through Jewish history basically in a short Talmudic account (*Shabbat* 21b). Aside from a few minor sources of limited circulation, the basic account of Hanukkah is reported thusly:

. . . on the 25th of Kislev [begin] the eight days of Hanukkah in which there are no mourning and no fasting. For when the Greeks entered the Temple they defiled all the oils in the Temple and when the Hasmonean monarchy grew in strength and overcame them they searched but found no more than one cruse of oil left — enough only for one day — with the seal of the High Priest. A miracle occurred and they were able to burn the lights (with that oil) for eight days. The following year, they established and designated these days as a holiday, with the recitation of Psalms (Hallel) and thanksgiving.

But there is more, much more to the story that speaks to us in our own times and in our own circumstances. The Hanukkah story itself took place around the year 167 BCE and some significant accounts of those events were written at the time. The Hebrew Bible, however, had already been officially completed in terms of the documents it contained and it was not possible to include the momentous events of Hanukkah therein. In addition, as the years went on, the dynasty of the victorious Hasmoneans became corrupt and pious religious authorities became less and less inclined to speak of the Hasmoneans despite the bravery and boldness of those earlier years. So, two things combined to render the Hanukkah story incomplete in ensuing years — the impossibility of including the Books of the Maccabees in the Bible and the reluctance of our Sages to give any extensive credit to a dynasty which had decayed. But, fortunately for us, the accounts of the Hanukkah story were preserved by those responsible for organizing and assembling the Christian Bible (how's that for irony?) and the Books of the Maccabees came down to us through history.

It is from the First Book of Maccabees that we gain insight into some quite significant information:

In those days there came forth *out of Israel* (here and throughout, my emphases [RAB]) lawless men who persuaded many, saying: 'let us go and make a covenant with the nations around us; for since we separated ourselves from them, many evils have come upon us.' That saying appeared good in their eyes and *certain of the people* went eagerly to the king who granted them authority to introduce the customs of the heathen . . . they submitted themselves to uncircumcision and repudiated the holy covenant; they joined themselves to the heathen and sold themselves to do evil.

Jewish society in Palestine was torn between those who urged steadfast loyalty to the customs, traditions and identity of the Jewish people (called Hasidim=Loyalists) and those (Hellenists=Assimilationists) who argued that the only way for Jews to secure their well-being in a non-Jewish world and bring an end to their suffering was to abandon those practices and folkways which encouraged Gentile repression and harshness (". . . for since we separated ourselves from them, many evils have befallen us.") So strongly did these Assimilationists feel, that they sought governmental enforcement of the prohibition against Jewish separatism:

Then the king wrote to his entire kingdom, that all should be one people, and that every one should give up his laws. All the nations acquiesced in accordance with the command of the king. *Even many in Israel* took delight in his worship and began sacrificing to idols and profaned the Sabbath. . . . Many of the people joined them, all those who had forsaken the Torah; *they* did evil in the land and caused the [loyal] Jews to hide in all manner of hiding places.

In their pursuit of the ideal of "being one people" and of becoming "like those around us among whom we live," the Assimilationists:

. . . offered sacrifices at the doors of the houses and in the streets. The books of the Torah which they found they tore into pieces and burned. With whomever was found a scroll of the Covenant, and if he was found consenting to the law of the Torah, he was, according to the king's sentence, condemned to death . . . they put to death the women who had circumcised their children . . . and put to death their families.

The Assimilationist fury was unleashed upon *fellow Jews* and conflict and repression continued for quite some time. It appeared that the Assimilationists would gain the upper hand until the emergence of a group of militant Loyalists, under Mattathias, who realized that, without armed resistance, authentic Jewish life would come to an end: .

> '. . . If we do not fight against the heathen for our lives and religion, they will soon destroy us from off the earth' . . . Then were gathered unto them a company of Loyalists, mighty men of Israel, each one offering himself willingly in defense of the Torah...they gathered an army and destroyed sinners in their anger, and lawless men in their wrath and the rest fled to the heathens to save themselves... Thus the Loyalists rescued the Torah from the hand of the heathens and the kings. . . .

As we, in our maturity now read and understand these things, we can say, with knowledge and conviction: NO! Hanukkah only *looks* like a holiday for children; the *real* Hanukkah is for US! NO! The truth of Jewish history is the TRUTH of Jewish history; if anything, it is far from fable and naive fantasy. NO! The sources of danger to our existence are NOT always outside us and, by knowing that, we may secure our collective lives. The decision and resolve of the Loyalists to actively oppose the Assimilationists and the imposition of royal repression was one of the most momentous events in Jewish history. The question was (and is) — which view should prevail? Is the answer to the difficulty of being Jewish in a Gentile world the shedding of Jewish practices which serve to separate us from others and bring us discriminatory grief, or is the Jewish response to a world asking us "to be like them" to hold more steadfastly onto our Torah, our values, our beliefs? It is crystal clear that had the Assimilationists won, we, as a Jewish people would not be here today (witness the disappearance of all those ancient peoples and nations who did forego their own cultures in favor of "The Greek Way"). It is equally clear that Jewish intransigence, stubbornness and refusal to give up our integrity and "knuckle under" have preserved and sustained monotheism, have "knuckle under" have preserved and sustained monotheism, have enabled Christianity (a message our Gentile friends would do well to ponder during the month of December!) and Islam to come into being and have perpetuated the values and norms of Torah for the perfection, not only of ourselves, but for the rest of the world.

For us, now, the question is, always, how shall we choose? Do we follow, often subtly but inexorably, after those of our people who believe that we must "be like the people around us" or do we endorse and support the voice in our history which argues that, ultimately, proud loyalty to Jewish life, values and practices preserves us, enhances our lives and benefits the entire world? Do we follow the doctrine which asserts that the source of our distress is THEM or rather do we declare our recognition of the truth that WE can be the enemy? Oil burning is not the only Hanukkah miracle — over two thousand years ago, we were able TO PREVAIL OVER OURSELVES AND SOME OF OUR OWN TENDENCIES — a miracle! — we prevailed over THE ENEMY WITHIN and for this, if for nothing else, Hanukkah draws us to its light and to its promise of a rich Jewish life through loyalty and affirmation and commitment!

SELF-INTEREST, DENIAL
AND JEWISH SOCIOLOGISTS

In my teaching and travelling around the country, I continue to be astonished (and saddened) by the pervasive orientation of our people to "truths" drawn from anecdote rather than formal assessment. My astonishment is made all the greater because I address educated and enlightened audiences who, for the most part, *in their own professions and arenas of intellectual functioning* would rarely base their assessments of reality (and, say, their consequent business plans) on hearsay and limited personal social interaction. Surveys and statistical assessments *are* important, and our own better judgement tells us, time and again, that thorough, sophisticated, scientific studies provide quite important windows into sober reality.

The Council of Jewish Federations 1990 National Jewish Population Survey (NJPS) is one of the most thorough, wide-ranging and well-constructed appraisals of American Jewry ever done and its data hold much significance for people who really care. Like so many excellent pieces of work however, I fear that both the data and their implications will be ignored (as they already are!) by many of the very people who are themselves manifestations of the problems we have been identifying in contemporary American Judaism. Another excellent piece of work (CMJS 8) has appeared which, utilizing data from the 1990 NJPS, focuses on the implications of that study for Jewish education.[53] Scientific appraisals of significant aspects of Jewish life and Jewish

---

[53] *When They Are Grown They Will Not Depart: Jewish Education and the Jewish Behavior of American Adults*, Sylvia Barack Fishman and Alice Goldstein, Research Report 8, Maurice and Marilyn Cohen Center for Modern Jewish Studies at Brandeis University and the Jewish Education Service of North America, March, 1993=(CMJS 8).

communal functioning are hard to come by but with the help of this latest publication, some very far-reaching implications for the future of the American Jewish community are now available.   I and others have claimed for a long time that, in terms of securing the future vitality and substance (and even census!) of the American Jewish community, day school education is the only way to go: a thorough, all-encompassing curricular and informal program which addresses the attention of the learner during *prime learning time;* a program which integrates the worlds of the secular and the Jewish in a natural, positive, symbiotic way; an environment which enhances the social interaction of Jews with Jews. Only the day school can do all these things and now, for the doubters, for the ill-informed, for the recalcitrant, scientifically-validated observations abound.

CMJS 8 works with four levels of Jewish educational intensity in organizing its observations, levels ranging from "NONE" to "SUBSTANTIAL (6+ YEARS OF SUPPLEMENTARY OR DAY SCHOOL)" and the assertion is made, early on, that ". . .*extensive Jewish education* is definitively associated with higher measures of adult Jewish identification (p.12)." Moreover, in four critical areas of Jewish life, the study notes, ". . . *extensive Jewish education* is related to a greater ritual observance, greater likelihood of belonging to and attending synagogues, greater levels of voluntarism for Jewish causes, and greater chances for marrying a Jew and being opposed to intermarriage among one's children (p.12)." Some illustrative figures are instructive here (I promise, no overwhelming with numbers): 26% of men and women, between the ages of 18 and 65+ have had *no* Jewish education at all and another 27.5% have had no more than Sunday School instruction (now living adult lives with an infantile training in and recall of Judaism! How many of these people are involved in policy formulation, decision-making and management in and for the Jewish community??) Conversely, among those with six or more years in a *day* school, 55.4% rated "High" on an index of ritual practice (as contrasted with only 14% of those who attended Hebrew School for 5 years!), more than 55% were synagogue members and a whopping 79% married born Jews. In the younger generation (25-44 years of age), only 34% of those with no Jewish education married born Jews and the Sunday School attenders averaged 42%.

The implications are clear: if we think that ritual and Jewish identity are necessary, fulfilling and important, if we believe that belonging to Jewish organizations and contributing to Jewish causes are good for the Jews and if we endorse the notion that our continuity as Jews in the wonderful, open, democratically pluralistic American society is linked with whom we choose to marry then there is no denying the figures — the odds for success are GREATLY improved through intensive *day school* education. Those who would deny this are simply attempting to cover their own weaknesses. Those who would cavil at the data assembled in the past few years are simply covering for their own failures and the Jewish poverty of their own family lives. We must beware of those in Jewish leadership positions who continue to appeal to anecdote in promoting anemic and pernicious public policy. Committed Jews are those who repudiate the pressures upon them to allow current social convention, self interest and assimilationist motivations to define what being a Jew means, whom one marries and how one lives (and *loves*). Those who truly care for the welfare of the Jewish people, in the context of the meaning of Jewish history, Jewish tradition and the perpetuation of Jewish values will attend carefully to what our demographers and social scientists are saying.

WHAT IF PESAH NEVER HAPPENED?

Aside from the biblical record itself, there is absolutely *no* evidence for the presence of Jews in ancient Egypt or their exodus therefrom. Despite Emanuel Velikovsky, Werner Keller and all the others who desperately seek and imagine clues which simply aren't there, the enslavement and ultimate liberation from Egypt are a record for the Torah only. Now don't get me wrong - for millenia, the Torah record has been sufficient for those who accept its truth. One can take no issue with any person for whom the truth of history is the truth revealed by scripture! But my concern here is with those for whom something more than Torah is needed to establish fact.

What shall we say about Pesah, this most central event in our history, when, for any of its details, large or small, we have no independent substantiation? To what can we appeal to demonstrate the reality of the Festival of Freedom? Perhaps, in the end, we will simply have to admit that Pesah never really happened at all! We have no archaeological proof, we have no anthropological proof, we have no liguistic proof, we have no corroborative literary proof.

But wait...who said that the only things which verify history are archaeology or anthropology or geology or things like that? Where did we ever get the idea that the truth of history is to be found in the armamentarium of the sciences? The Jewish tradition would assert that the TRUTH of history is not its independently verifiable data but rather its *consequentiality,* that history is *what it has come to mean in the lives of people who take it seriously.* The Jewish people have taken Pesah seriously and an entire legal/behavioral system has grown up around the TRUTH that Pesah happened. Every time we say that the alien must not be oppressed (*Exodus* 23:9), we verify that Pesah happened —

Do not oppress an alien; you yourselves know how
it feels to be aliens, because you were aliens in
Egypt.

All the while we eat matzah during the festival (*Exodus*
12:17-18), we confirm that Pesah happened —
Celebrate the Feast of Unleavened Bread, because it
was on this very day that I brought your ranks out
of Egypt. Celebrate this day as a lasting ordinance
for your generations to come . . . you shall eat
unleavened bread . . .

All the while we reject slavery (*Leviticus* 25:39-42), we
establish the truth of our history —
If one of your countrymen becomes poor among you
and sells himself to you, do not work him as a slave
. . . because the Israelites are my servants, whom I
liberated from Egypt, they must not be sold as
slaves.

All the while we raise up our children in the Jewish
tradition (*Exodus* 12:26-27), we substantiate the reality of our past
experience—
And when your children ask you, "What do you
mean by this rite?" you shall say, "It is the Pesah
sacrifice to the Lord who protected the houses of the
Israelites in Egypt when he struck the Egyptians but
saved our houses. . . ."

All the while we pursue holiness (*Leviticus* 11:45), we attest
to God and God's providence in history —
I am the Lord who brought you up out of Egypt to
be your God; therefore be holy, because I am holy.

In all, for us it is not the matter that we *speak* of history, it
is the matter that we *live* it! Our daily actions, our private lives,
our mundane behaviors, our professional conduct — all relate
somehow and someway to the ultimate truths which *we* have the

power to validate. The Torah instructs us, in speaking of weights and measures (*Leviticus* 19:35-37) —

> You shall not falsify measures of length, weight or capacity. You shall have an honest balance, honest weights, an honest ephah and an honest hin. I the Lord am your God who freed you from the land of Egypt. You shall faithfully observe all My laws and all My rules; I am the Lord.

And our teacher Moses Maimonides in his sublime legal code, *Mishneh Torah*, sums up for us the essence of the verity and reality of history for Jews (*Torts, Theft*, 7:12) —

> Whoever denies the binding validity [of the commandment relating to] measures, denies in effect the Exodus from Egypt, which is the basis of the commandment; but whoever obligates himself to the commandment relating to measures, acknowledges thereby the Exodus from Egypt, which rendered all the commandments possible.

Anyone who thinks Pesah never really happened simply hasn't been doing anything about it!

THOU SHALT NOT FORGET

The colloquialism "forgive and forget" causes me no end of anguish. The fact is, the concept of linking forgiveness and forgetting is a distinctly non-Jewish one and constitutes another significant intrusion of the Gentile world into authentic Jewish values. The celebration of Purim is, in the final analysis, the celebration of memory and the redemptive power of historical recollection. It is worth noting that the Shabbat before Purim is designated *Shabbat Zachor* (the Sabbath of "Remember!") and that a special Torah reading (*Deuteronomy* 25:17-19) is conducted at that time:

> Remember what Amalek did to you on your journey, after you left Egypt — how, undeterred by fear of God, he surprised you on the march, when you were famished and weary, and cut down all the stragglers in your rear. Therefore, when the Lord your God grants you safety from all your enemies around you, in the land that the Lord your God is giving you as a hereditary portion, you shall blot out the memory of Amalek from under heaven. Do not forget!

Our tradition enjoins us to read this passage as a mitzvah! It is a matter of religious obligation and, in reading it, we are regarded as fulfilling the commandment to REMEMBER. The public reading of this passage is one of the 613 mitzvot which comprise the behavioral matrix of Judaism and it is indeed remarkable, and probably unique in the universe of religious traditions, that merit is gained through the conscious remembering of a historical event and its significance. Our Tradition teaches us that the villain Haman, from the story of Esther, was a descendent of this selfsame Amalek and, in further fulfillment of the

Deuteronomic passage, noisemakers are sounded at the mention of his name during the reading of the Scroll of Esther ("you shall blot out"). Observe however, a remarkable paradox! We are enjoined to "blot out the memory of Amalek. . ." and, at the same time, are told "Do not forget." How are we to explain this remarkable incongruity? We are bidden both to recall the details and directed to eradicate the memory of the perpetrator.

The story of Esther is a reminder that the villainy of history can always reappear, in another time, in another place, in another mask, but if we are to be able to recognize it, in order to oppose it, then we must have retained a keen reminiscence of our past. Without the recollection of the past, we are powerless to identify the mortal threats of the present. Mordecai knew his past well (that's why we are given his genealogy back to Kish, father of King Saul ([*Esther* 2:5]) and he made sure, as Esther's guardian, that she knew who she was (2:10). Haman's demands upon Mordecai (3:5) and subsequent intention to eradicate all the Jews (3:6) sounded familiar and impelled Mordecai (with his strategy) and Esther (with her very *body*) to do what was necessary to save the Jewish people. The Scroll of Esther is about history, about consequentiality, about the *redemptive power of memory* (is that why our Sages have said that, in the era of the Messiah, all the holidays will be set aside *except* Purim?).

One of the great gifts we wish to give the world is this sense of the meaning of memory. Austria is still unredeemed. It was able to elect Kurt Waldheim president because it had no sense of his, and Austria's past. For most Austrians, the Holocaust did not happen. Innocent Turks, along with other "foreigners", can be beaten and burned alive in the Germany of today because there is no compelling coming to terms with the Germany of yesterday. Reparations for survivors and warm relations with Israel still do not begin to equal what we would call *memory* and without a memory people can propose building convents at Auschwitz and selling poison gas to Iraq.

Of all the world's people we do not have to be taught to forgive. It is Judaism which developed and formulated the concept of expiation (*kippur*) through repentance (*teshuva*), for the idea that human behavior is alterable, reparable and perfectible. But our concept of *teshuva* requires not only that we firmly resolve never again to repeat the wrongful act, but that we keep an indelible mental and spiritual record of where we have been!

There can be no defense against evil without the conditioning of history which enables us to identify it. There can be no forgiveness for crime without the recall of its commission. Despite all the wonderful good and monumental vision of something like Pope Paul VI's "Declaration on the Relation of the Church to Non-Christian Religions" (October 28, 1965), the repudiation of antisemitism and the recognition of the validity of Judaism notwithstanding, the phrase "...this sacred synod urges all to forget the past . . ." calls to mind our unfinished task to engage the rest of the world in the celebration of the ultimate Purim.

"RELIEF AND DELIVERANCE WILL COME TO THE JEWS FROM ANOTHER QUARTER"

Just when we think we finally understand, things are turned on their heads. You just never really know! That's what Purim is all about — you just never really know and what you do know is very likely to be something else. Purim is a great time for reassessing our verities and our certainties, a wonderful occasion for celebrating the absurdity of it all. What you think you see isn't always what you get and just when you think the game is up, you get a chance to start all over again.

The Book of Esther (*not* the Book of Mordecai, by the way!) is replete with inversions, reversals and transpositions (the only other biblical book named for a woman is Ruth, the story of an outsider who becomes an insider, as contrasted with Esther who is an insider living like an outsider!!). Sometimes all you can do is just laugh, and we do a *lot* of laughing on Purim and, in fact, a lot of laughing for the whole month of Adar ("When Adar comes around, we are exceedingly happy"[54]). In a way, Purim is a metaphor for life, for the unexpected, the unforseen. We laugh a lot on Purim because we escaped death by the skin of our teeth.[55] Among other things, Purim is a celebration of the ludicrous in our lives (corporate lives, to be sure) and it's no wonder we wear masks and don costumes — what a wonderful way to say "now you see it, now you don't." Sometimes the world is topsy-turvy and sometimes it all ends well.

The next time you read the Book of Esther (yes, the whole megillah), you might want to look for these inversions and then

---

[54] *Babylonian Talmud, Ta'anit* 29a.

[55] A wonderful biblically-derived expression, see *Job* 19:20.

search for more on your own. Consider that the once submissive Vashti finally learns to say "No!" and that the very chaste Esther finally says "Yes!" The reviled Jew, Mordecai, becomes the object of Haman's homage and the horse which Haman had imagined for himself becomes Mordecai's instead (sorry!). Just because you're a eunuch (like Hathach) doesn't mean you've lost everything and he who once had everything (like Haman) ends up with nothing. The stake prepared for impaling the Jew ultimately becomes Haman's hangup and the royal signet which sealed the decree of death becomes the seal on the license to life. Antisemites become Jews and closet Jews go public. The month for lamentation becomes the month for joy and he who laughs first comes in last.

Then, just when you think you've got a good handle on all the reversals and transpositions, yet a few more hit you and these may be the biggest yet! Almost all of biblical literature takes place in and focuses upon Eretz Yisrael but this story takes place in the Diaspora. Most all the biblical heroes are men, but here it is a woman who saves the day. All the Jewish holidays are bound up with Israel, Purim remains in the Exile. And an Esther who was well assimilated into the life of the Gentile world becomes the key to the saving of the Jews of Persia - an Esther many would have rejected as perhaps too secular or too "Gentile" or too much like the kept women around her. The periphery becomes the core and the margin becomes the center. After all is said and done, Purim reminds us that *all* Jews are dear and precious and that none of us can ever know with a certainty who will and who will not come to the aid and deliverance of our people. "Do not reject anyone and do not consider anything impossible, for there is no person who has not his hour and no thing that does not have its place."[56]

---

[56] *Chapters of the Sages*, 4:3; part of the Mishnaic literature of the first several centuries of the Common Era and characterized by its profound and singular focus on pietism.

TRUTH AND CONSEQUENCES

One of the most outstanding characteristics of the Jewish tradition, from the time of Torah on, is the unrelenting view that all phenomena which occur in our universe are interrelated, whether we readily see those relationships or not. It is this understanding that is reflected in the idea that all significant events *will* have significant consequences. Judaism has, from the very beginning, dismissed the notions of luck or accident or irrelevance in assessing the meaning of life and of human affairs. *Consequentiality* is the keyword and, ultimately, the key concept in urging us consistently to assess our behaviors, measure the scope of our actions and live our lives in the context of our ability to make choices and the inescapable effects which result from those choices. The very moral substance of the Jewish people, through Torah, is manifest in our refusal to see life and the things we live for as anything other than response to our application of choice, of vision, of commitment, of *neshamah* (a Hebrew/Yiddish term, loosely translated as "soul").

Every choice we make has significance, every investment we make has consequence and every present moment has future implication. For us and for the Torah institutions we build, then becomes now, today is tomorrow and this world is the entrance hall for the world to come. This is our substance, this is our identity, this is what we are and this is what we want to be. This is why we are a unique and Godly people and this is what we want the world to emulate. This is the meaning of our lives, and this is what makes life worth living. In one of the most elegant passages ever written, our Sages encapsulated meaning and purpose and cause and effect and act and consequence in a way sublimely giving voice to something we always have known:

> . . . If there are no children, there will be no adults
> and if there are no adults there will be no Sages; if

there are no Sages, there will be no Prophets and if there are no Prophets there will be no Holy Spirit; if there is no Holy Spirit there will be no synagogues and academies - in effect, God will not cause his Presence to dwell upon Israel. [*Jerusalem Talmud, Sanhedrin* 51a]

GODLINESS

"God created Man in His own image, in the image of God He created him; male and female He created them"
[Genesis 1:27]

"BE A MENSCH!" — DYNAMIC TORAH

It seems to me that we rarely take the time these days to devote some serious thought to just what we're all about in terms of the behavioral expectations our tradition addresses to us. In a certain sense, chagrin for this failure is made all the greater as we observe the continuing precipitous decline, in America, of the kinds of values we have long believed are necessary for maintaining a healthy society. Our tradition does have much to offer by way of addressing concepts of decent behavior, goodness, honesty. Our long existence as a people has made us the heirs of a rich set of experiences and we owe it to ourselves, perhaps now more than ever, to repeat to ourselves the things we have always known but which are waiting to be rediscovered.

I suppose we have all had the experience, in some conversation with someone unfamiliar with Jewish civilization, of using a Hebrew (or more likely, Yiddish) term and then quickly apologizing for the fact that the term "simply cannot be translated!" Many are the times, I imagine, when a particular Jewish cultural term seemed the *perfect* expression to use in some conversation or other and we paused, ever so slightly, to reflect on the fact that there was no really good way of expressing ourselves in English. Well, that's what this essay is all about — how to begin to find the words for expressing and explaining (primarily to ourselves, and then to others) some ideas of great substance and significance. I've been thinking a lot lately about *menschlichkeit* — recently I met a few *menschen* and I was lamenting the fact that there are so few around.

Your dictionaries won't help you a lot here. Alexander Harkavy's classic *Yiddish-English Verterbukh* renders "mensch" as "man, employee, servant" and the abstract noun "menschlichkeit" as "humanity, human nature." Those renderings don't even begin to tell the story. German dictionaries (the word is German in origin) aren't much better — check them out and you'll find, for *mensch,* something like "human being" — rather far from the mark (no fiscal pun intended), isn't it? Yet, for some of us, defining *menschlichkeit* is somewhat like the Supreme Court Justice who said, regarding pornography "I can't define it but I know it when I see it!" Well, that's nice but...how do you explain it, anyway. As is so often the case in these pages, our classic tradition has some powerful things to say about the whole matter and while you won't exactly find the word itself used, as you read and contemplate, you have no doubt about what we have meant throughout the ages:

> What does the Torah mean when it says: "You shall follow after the Lord your God" [*Deuteronomy,* 13:4]? Is it really possible for a person to walk in the Divine Presence, considering that the Torah says: "The Lord thy God is a consuming fire" [*Deuteronomy,* 4:24]? In reality, the meaning is that we are to follow the *attributes* of God: Just as He clothed the naked [Adam and Eve in the Garden of Eden], so shall *you* clothe the naked; just as He visited the sick [Abraham, after his circumcision], so shall *you* visit the sick; as He comforted mourners [Isaac, after the death of his father], so shall *you* comfort those who mourn and as He buried the dead [Moses], so shall *you* bury the dead. (*Babylonian Talmud, Sotah* 14a)

One of the most significant things that can be said about the Jewish concept of *menschlichkeit* is that it never propounds a behavior which is not clearly within the realm of reasonable expectation for performance. Our tradition *never* sets up as a virtue the doing of an act which is alien to the general abilities of people. The behaviors for which we are being exhorted are reasonable, doable and definitive. Some other traditions with which we might be familiar ask, for example, that we "love our enemies" or that, "when slapped in the face, turn the other cheek" — responses which contradict the generality of human nature and which, therefore, are more likely to be honored in the breech than in the observance. Moreover, equally important, and so exquisitely Jewish is the fact that *menschlichkeit* is *always* an act and *never* a feeling! *Behaviors* can be demanded but *feelings* can't.

Having said that, it is important to note that *menschlichkeit* is not a Jewish monopoly. Gentiles as well as Jews can be *menschen* and the qualities represented by *menschlichkeit* are available to all. A famous story in the Talmud used to illustrate the point that we Jews are not singular in the understanding of what it means to honor parents, reports:

> Go forth and see what a certain heathen, Dama ben Netina by name, did in Ashkelon. The Sages sought gems for the priestly garment at a profit of 600,000 dinars but as the key [to the jewel box] was lying under his father's pillow, he did not disturb him. The following year, God rewarded him [for his meritorious act] and a valuable red heifer was born to his herd. The Sages came to purchase the animal [for Temple use] and he said to them: I know that even if I asked all the money in the world, you would give it to me for this red heifer. But I ask only for the money I lost through honoring my father. (*Babylonian Talmud, Qiddushin* 31a)

Women as well as men can be *menschen* (an exquisite non-sexist term!) and children too can bear this title and all people can be the beneficiaries of *menschlichkeit*:

> Our Rabbis have taught: We must support the poor of the Gentiles with the poor of Israel, visit the sick of the Gentiles with the sick of Israel and give honorable burial to the dead of the Gentiles as to the dead of Israel, because of the ways of peace.[57] (*Babylonian Talmud, Gittin* 61a)

The concept of "the ways of peace" [*mipne darkhe shalom*]

---

[57] Notice how remarkably similar this is to *Sotah* 14a, above!

is a wide-reaching value in Judaism and, among other things, it addresses itself to the idea that *defined* interpersonal social behavior can make the world better:

> Benevolence *(gemilut hasadim)* is greater than almsgiving in three respects: almsgiving is performed with money but benevolence is performed with personal service or money; almsgiving is restricted to the poor but benevolence can be done to poor and rich; almsgiving can be done only to the living but benevolence can be done for the living and the dead.[58] *(Babylonian Talmud, Sukkah* 49b)

Another rather remarkable aspect of our concept of *menschlichkeit* is that it may be evidenced even out of *profound self-interes*t!:

> Said Rabbi Akiva . . . What is hateful to you do not do to another. If you wish that no one harm you in connection with what belongs to you, you must not harm another in that way; if you wish that no one deprive you of what is yours, you must not deprive another of what belongs to him. *(Avot d'Rabbi Natan* 26)

So important is the idea of *menschlichkeit* and so critical is it for maintaining a civilized society that Jewish tradition does not shirk at all from urging that, if all else fails, then pure self-interest can be made to express itself in positive ways. We see then, on the basis of the illustrations here alone, that *menschlichkeit* can be spoken of in three modes: firstly, it may be thought of as imitating God (= Godliness); secondly, it may be thought of as promoting social harmony and lastly, it can even be conceptualized as the practice of benign egotism! Three kinds of *menschlichkeit* for three kinds of people, "different strokes for different folks" you might say, with no excuses possible for non-performance. That's something of the essence of a behavioral system, a system which

---

[58] As in assisting in a burial, as mentioned above.

is Judaism's leading characteristic and perhaps even the essence of its uniqueness.

> If you have done another a little wrong, let it be great in your eyes; if you have done another much good, let it be little in your eyes; if another has done you a little good, let it be much in your eyes and if another has done you a great wrong, let it be in your eyes as little. (*Avot d'Rabbi Natan* 41)

FROM THE ORDINARY TO THE EXTRAORDINARY

To the religious mind, all of nature is available for being made "sacred," including geographical areas, localized spaces within buildings . . . people, and even time itself.   [*Mircea Eliade*[59], 140]

As the period of Rosh Hashanah and Yom Kippur approaches, even the so-called "non-religious" among us somehow sense that the "High Holidays" are special and important. We have learned that human beings, throughout the ages and across all cultural and geographical boundaries, exhibit many shared spiritual characteristics and that among these are the need for experiencing sacredness and the need for exercising some kind of control over Time (which, we used to say, "waits for no man"). We want to know, somehow, that we are not mere specks of cosmic dust, meaningless and insignificant to an uncaring and undifferentiating universe. We want to know that our lives, our loves, our small *personal* universes *do* count for something, that what we live *for* can be vastly different from what we *do* for a living. We want to know that we are not always prisoners of routine and creatures of predictable, predetermined usualness. We *have* to have at least a periodic taste of the "could be" and a touch of the "might be." Stained souls need cleansing and failed ambitions need some consolation. Missed opportunities and awkward foulups need second chances; spirits in disrepair need some time to rest and recuperate. We need each other. That's what synagogue (temple, shul, whatever you call it) is *really* all about.

---

[59] All Eliade citations are from *Myths, Rites, Symbols: A Mircea Eliade Reader*, vol. 1, edited by Wendell C. Beane and William G. Doty, Harper Collophon Books, 1976.

Growing up I too was part of the chorus ridiculing all those three-day-a-year Jews flocking to shul in their finest clothing, ready to submit themselves to as much as five or six hours of "please rise, please be seated, turn to page such-and-such, let us read responsively." There was a time when I was certain that the emptiness of it all was laughable. And you know, it didn't make a bit of difference...the people still came in droves and continued to submit themselves to hallowed recitation and choreography. Some, to be sure, stayed away, overwhelmed by the chimera of "hypocrisy" and driven by the pervasive non-Jewish notion that "if you don't do it all, you really shouldn't be doing any." And there were always the stalwart ones, the intellectually liberated who just knew that this kind of annual reverence was really for the unenlightened, non-thinking masses (masses still rendered insensate by the opiate of religion). *Real* people don't mumble unintelligible words and dance "stand up, sit down" sacral choreographs. . . .

Then some of us grew up, some of us even discovered Mircea Eliade and Mordecai Kaplan and the worlds of serious religion and cultural anthropology and the human sciences. We discovered that more people are religious than care to see it in themselves; that more people need religion than are ready to admit it and that more truths surround us than we have been conditioned to perceive. We discovered that, *for Jews,* simply being together with other Jews at a Jewish time and in a Jewish place for a Jewish purpose is an enormously satisfying, authentic spiritual moment. We discovered that it is *we* who make Rosh Hashanah and Yom Kippur:

> The [Rabbinical] Court decreed: "Today is the New Year." The Holy One, Blessed be He said to the Ministering Angels: 'Erect the courtroom stand and let both the defense and the prosecution come forth, for My children have decreed that today is Rosh Hashanah.' The Court, after more consideration, calculated [that the New Year would begin] on the *next day.* The Holy One, Blessed be He said to the Ministering Angels: 'Remove the courtroom stand and let the defense and prosecution depart for My children have decided to set [the New Year] for

tomorrow.' [*Palestinian Talmud, Rosh Hashanah* 1:3]

We discovered our ability to transcend time, to make yomtov in a non-yomtov world, to make Jewish in a non-Jewish world. To make Saturday into Shabbat and September into Tishre. To make edifice into synagogue, to make not eating into fasting and to make fasting into Jewish-connection and to make Jewish-connection into God-connection. We discovered all kinds of powers and prerogatives and potentials we didn't really know we had:

> . . . [religious] man does not accept the irreversibility of Time . . . ritual abolishes profane, chronological Time and recovers sacred Time . . . this revolt against the irreversibility of Time helps man to "construct reality" . . . it frees him from the weight of dead Time, assures him that he is able to abolish the past, to begin his life anew, and to re-create his world. . . . [*Mircea Eliade,* 138-9]

We discovered our ability to transform the ordinary into the extraordinary and we discovered the great satisfaction and fulfillment in such transformation. We discovered that Torah can be a handbook for performing these transformations and that the more we engage in transformation, the more we remind ourselves that we are alive. We discovered that apples and honey are far more than food, that a festive meal is far more than eating and that dressing up goes way beyond "showing off." We discovered that holding a prayerbook can be as significant as reading it and that kiddush can turn wine into history:

> Rituals are symbols in acted reality; they function to make concrete and experiential the mythic values of a society, and they can therefore provide clues to the mythic values themselves. Hence, rituals *act*, they perform, modulate, transform . . . Rituals form the patterns of life and . . . provide periodic re-creation of the world, of potency . . . Rituals are also

significant as a means of maintaining a sense of the
sacred. . . . [*Mircea Eliade,* 164]

Our Sages of millennia ago prefigured Eliade and the
human sciences. They too marvelled at the enormous wonderment
of being Jewish, of being endowed with an *awareness* of
specialness, of purpose, of personal and communal significance.
They saw in us all, through the lens of Torah, the divine ability to
enrich our lives with sacredness and to master time, to transform
ourselves, our families, our communities, even for a moment, into
a taste of what "could be" and into a touch of what "might be":

> What blessing should one make when he sees the
> new moon? When Israel used to sanctify the new
> month, some of our Rabbis would say "Blessed is
> He who makes new months." But there were those
> of them who would say "Blessed is He who
> sanctifies the months." Some would say "Blessed is
> He who sanctifies Israel", for if Israel does not
> sanctify it, its sanctification means nothing. Do not
> be astonished by this for the Holy One Blessed be
> He sanctified Israel, as it is said [*Leviticus* 20:26]:
> "You shall be holy unto Me because I God am holy"
> and since Israel is holy to God, WHATEVER
> THEY SANCTIFY IS HOLY. . . .[*Exodus Rabbah,
> Bo,* 24]

ACCESSIBLE HOLINESS:
WORKING FOR THE JEWISH COMMUNITY

One of the disabilities we suffer living in a Gentile world is that we have been deeply and wrongly influenced in our notion of what is meant by the term "religion." I would venture to say that, in our society, most people, Jews and Gentiles alike, think, consciously or unconsciously, that "religion" (and related things, like "holiness") are associated essentially with worship and ritual. That this is so should not be very surprising in light of Western civilization's popular understanding of religion.[60] As we have discussed, this prevailing understanding has impacted heavily upon Jews and has been responsible, sadly, for our increasing failure to see something of the virtue of our own civilization. In the main, even our parents and our Hebrew school teachers,[61] all in their own ways, reinforced this notion. We have failed, in large measure, to see God and religiosity and holiness as much more significant parts of our lives than might be immediately apparent.

It is precisely because Judaism is not a religion but a civilization and because all the component parts of that civilization inform and interact with each other, that we Jews come into contact so much more frequently with manifestations of things Godly and religious. Since Biblical times, our basic unit of civilizational

---

[60] See *Judaism Is More Than A Religion*, pp.11ff.

[61] Interesting, isn't it, how the institutions many of us attended were called *Hebrew* schools or *Sunday* schools; the former focusing on a language designation (like a Jewish Berlitz) and the latter, *a direct borrowing from Christianity,* focusing on context rather than content?!

meaning has always been the *group*[62] (and minimum group is *family*, consisting, look out America, of a father and a mother and children!) — not the individual. The concept of "Covenant" (see *English Is A Christian Language,* pp.22ff. and *Why Be Jewish?,* pp.48ff.) has always applied to the *corporate* Jewish people; all the blessings and curses, all the rewards and punishments articulated in the Bible as provisions of Covenant apply *only* to the entirety of the people. Individual acts, the propriety of which is expounded by Torah, are judged and responded to by human agency, not by the divine. Always and in every instance, our sense of history and of purpose has been collective. We understand act and consequence, reward and punishment, to be societal, not individual. Given our understanding of the intimate relationship between God and the Jewish people then, it follows that involvement with group and definition through group would occupy the highest level of significance and meaning. A wonderful passage in our literature exclaims, quite astonishingly: "[Elijah was travelling from place to place and met a man who said to him], 'Master, there are two things in my heart which I love greatly, Torah and the Jewish people, but I don't know which of them takes precedence.' "I said to him, 'People generally say that Torah takes precedence over everything . . . but I would say that the Jewish people take precedence, because they are holy.'"[63]

That is why we said, many centuries ago: "It is forbidden for a person to place his own prayer ahead of that of the

---

[62]   An engaging narrative from the first century of the Common Era says this so well: "Thus taught Rabbi Shimon ben Yohai: 'Men were sitting in a boat, one of them took a drill and began to bore a hole in the floor under his feet. His fellow passengers said to him: "What are you doing?" He responded: "What is it your matter, am I not drilling a hole under my own seat?" "Yes, but when the water comes it will drown all of us in the boat!" [*Vayikra Rabbah* 4]

[63]   *Tanna deBey Eliyahu,* ed. Ish Shalom, section 14, chapter 15 (p.71). It is highly significant that , in our post-biblical literature, Elijah is almost always portrayed as being a direct agent of God! This work is an assemblage of wise observations, Torah commentary and pietistic narrative, some of the composition of which is two thousand years old. Like other midrash of this type and period, this work is a beautiful and compelling window into the thinking and sensitivities of classical Judaism.

community."[64] That is why, many centuries ago, we said: "The presence of God is immanent only in *community.*"[65]

When we speak of "holiness" then, in the real and authentic Jewish sense of the term, we mean: *The perception that the mundane and commonplace can be invested with meaning, significance, purpose and Godliness and that these factors can enhance the quality and satisfaction of life for one's self and for others.* The Torah teaches: "You shall be for Me a kingdom of priests, a *holy people*" (*Exodus* 19:6). In the logic of Jewish history and in the mindset of the Jewish people, to be involved with and to contribute, in some way, to the well-being and care of the Jewish people is *holy* work and access to such holiness virtually surrounds us in our daily lives. And since Judaism is primarily *behavioral* and only secondarily doctrinal, the door to holiness, and hence to Godliness, is always open. Now we can understand the wonderful depths of meaning in the saying, "One who is involved with the needs of the community is the same as one who is involved in Torah."[66]

Our commitment to community is tantamount to our commitment to Torah and our commitment to Torah is tantamount to our commitment to God.[67] The exercising of that commitment makes us at one even with our greatest heroes: "At the time when the community is immersed in difficulty, let not a person say: 'I will go to my house and I will eat and I will drink and I will be alright' — rather, everyone must share the tribulation of the community, for thus we see in Torah that Moses our teacher shared fully the distress of the community-at-large."[68] And, as if to insure that individual burden not become an impediment in the doing of

---

[64] *Babylonian Talmud, Berachot* 28a.

[65] *Seder Olam* 15.

[66] *Jerusalem Talmud, Berachot* 5:1.

[67] This is *precisely* what is meant by the classical remark, "God, Torah and Israel are one." [*Zohar, Vayikra,* 73]

[68] *Babylonian Talmud, Ta'anit* 11a.

holiness, we remind ourselves: "The burden of the community is a heavy burden and no single person is able to bear it alone; know thou that even Moses, the master of all the Prophets, was not able to bear the burden of the community by himself."[69]

In the final analysis, it is community which enables us to have access not only to holiness, but to Godliness itself, and so to our own souls. It is our own tradition and the things we have always been saying to ourselves which call to mind the noble purposes we serve as we serve each other. We are reminded that our labors on behalf of fellow Jews, whatever those labors may be, are holy labors and that our religiosity and embrace of God are deeper and more substantial and more pervasive than those who do not understand us will ever know!:

> Just as God is called "Compassionate" so must you be compassionate. Just as God is called "Merciful" so must you be merciful. Just as God is called "Holy" so must you be holy. In this manner our prophets referred to God with the epithets "Patient," "Generous," "Righteous," "Honest," "Blameless," "Heroic," "Strong," . . . to teach that these are good and proper characteristics of behavior and that we are obligated to conduct ourselves with these qualities and attempt to imitate God as much as we can. (Maimonides, *Mishneh Torah, Knowledge*, 1)[70]

---

[69] *Devarim Rabbah* 1:7. This statement is built, among others, upon the narrative in the Torah, *Exodus* 18:13-23: "The next day, Moses sat as magistrate among the people and the people stood about Moses from morning until night. But when (Jethro) Moses' father-in-law saw how much he had to do for the people, he said, 'Why do you act alone . . . what you are doing is not right, you will wear yourself out...because the task is too burdensome for you; you cannot do it alone . . . search out from among all the people capable men who revere God . . . and let them judge the people . . . and let them share the burden with you...*that is God's will. . . .'"

[70] Maimonides based this, in large part, upon *Sifre, Deuteronomy,* sec. 49 and it is this source which says directly: "How is it possible for a person to have direct access (lit. "to call upon") to God? Just as God is compassionate, so shall you be..." *Sifre* is a collection of Rabbinic/Tannaitic homilies and expositions on the Torah books of *Numbers* and *Deuteronomy*. These sources are valuable for the insight they provide into Jewish thought processes and values in the first several centuries of the Common era.

INDEX